How
to
Hold On

Ten Strategies to Save Your Marriage

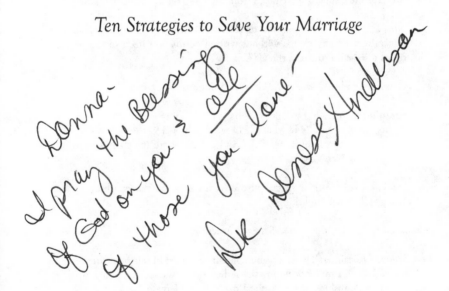

Donna—
I pray the Blessings
of God on you & all
of those you love!
Dr. Denese Anderson

Dr. Denese Anderson

Trilogy Christian Publishers
A Wholly Owned Subsidiary of Trinity Broadcasting Network
2442 Michelle Drive
Tustin, CA 92780

Cover design by: Cornerstone Creative Solutions

For information, address Trilogy Christian Publishing
Rights Department, 2442 Michelle Drive, Tustin, Ca 92780.
Trilogy Christian Publishing/ TBN and colophon are trademarks of Trinity Broadcasting Network.

For information about special discounts for bulk purchases, please contact Trilogy Christian Publishing.

Manufactured in the United States of America

10 9 8 7 6 5 4 3 2 1

Library of Congress Cataloging-in-Publication Data is available.

ISBN 978-1-63769-012-3 (Print Book)
ISBN 978-1-63769-013-0 (ebook)

CONTENTS

Acknowledgments

In a lifelong journey for healthy relationships, I've studied the art of connection. I have lived, I have loved, and I have lost. Through this journey and my education, I have discovered many techniques that are effective in building successful relationships. My hope is the information gathered in this book will help you achieve success in your relationships as well.

I am a Christian, a mother, a wife, a counselor, a friend, and a person who cares for others and their good health. The Lord has blessed me with great friends, a wonderful family, great pastors, and some of the best educators there are available. I must give thanks to Him first and foremost.

I am also thankful that I was blessed with godly grandparents who taught me the ways and foundations of a godly life. I will carry them in my heart until I meet them again in heaven.

The Lord blessed my life the day He brought Kurt Anderson into it. Kurt has taught me all I know about real and lasting love. He is my beacon of light in this often unkind world. I treasure his love more than words can express; he is my true love. I thank God for a journey of ups and downs. I am thankful for every minute we have together.

The Lord blessed me with three motherly figures that gave me all I needed to become the woman I am today. First, I must thank my mother, Ellen Wilson. She was hard-working, truthful, and always ready with love when it was needed. She taught me I can do anything, and I do not have to live within the limits others want to set for me. Second, I want to thank Cathy Holman, my aunt. She has led me to understand the way others communicate and all the different ways we show our love. Aunt Cathy, you have blessed my life with your wisdom, love, and guidance. I love you and will forever be grateful to all you sowed into my life. Last but certainly not least, for my Dr. Mom, Dr. MR Burckley-Frost. She was my mentor, professor, and dearest friend. She now lives in heaven with Jesus, and I miss her every day. She is the one that showed me my gifts and how they could be used in the counseling office. She held my hand as I honed my calling and skills. She loved me when I failed, she praised me when I succeeded, and most importantly, she cheered me on when I needed support. These three great women have taught me to be authentically me and celebrated who I became. I thank God for them and their effects on my life daily.

I am thankful for all three of my wonderful children and my two grandchildren. Thank you all for loving me even when I didn't get everything right. Thank you for your support and care and all the days it was needed. I love you all so very much, and I'm grateful to God for this family that He created.

A special note of thanks to all the dear friends of faith that have been there for me when I needed to cry, laugh, praise, or play. Cathie, you have been an amazing friend for a lifetime. For that, I thank you. Cyndi, you have held my hand and let me weep, laugh, or just vent. Thank you, dear friend. I love you. Linda, thank you for your encouragement and prayers; you truly have prayed this book into existence. And for the dear, sweet Jasmyne, thank you for your wonderful art skills, you are a special jewel in my life, and I appreciate and love you very much.

Thank you to all the successful marriages that have taught me how to work through the difficult moments to get to the great ones. You encouraged me to work towards the best possible marriage and never give up trying.

I have learned so much from every couple I have worked with in the counseling office through the last sixteen years. Thank you to each one who trusted me when they were seeking better health in their relationships. Thank you for all I have learned from all of you.

To God be the glory for any marriages restored, any love brought back to life, and for any understanding obtained within this book. He is the true author of this book, and all knowledge comes from Him.

Introduction

When relationships begin, they generally start with desire, interest, and excitement of new beginnings. Then time brings us closer, and relationships grow through the different seasons of our lives and sometimes patience and understanding for one another can change. This book was written to assist development in your level of closeness and communication. The intention is to bring understanding for common behaviors and reactions you may be experiencing within your marriage. Most partners need to further develop their lines and methods of communication. This book has simple to use concepts that will usher in forgiveness, acceptance, and a deeper understanding that your spouse processes differently than you do and what that means for your marriage. With this understanding and acceptance of your differences, love will grow and flourish to deeper and deeper levels. It is completely possible for your marriage to get better and better each year you are together.

All normal marriages have their challenging moments or seasons. Generally, couples experience times of closeness and heated passion, as well as times of misunderstandings. There are also times of frustration and unmet needs. To have a successful marriage, you must have the ability to navigate all the above. This is the meaning behind this book—to help you navigate the challenges of life together as a successful team.

In my experience of marriage counseling, I have found there are ten key factors that I work on repeatedly with couples in therapy. These key factors are outlined within this book with clear strategies of how you can apply them to your relationship. It is common when you are first learning the strategies for it to feel like work. However, if you stick with them and make them your habit, they will bring your marriage great benefits.

Value Levels and Successful Connections

First and foremost, we must honestly evaluate the value levels you place on your priorities. It has always been interesting to me that when you ask people about their priorities, they generally answer with their priority list. We associate with listing the aspect of duties, requirements, and wants in order of priority. We each make choices daily as to what we put at the top of our list. In the counseling office, I often hear someone describing where they are on their mate's priority list. Whether it be the top or bottom of the list can tell you much about their relationship quality. Each person in your life has a value level where they fall on your priority list. It directly reflects the amount of time and intention you apply to the relationship.

As I was growing up, I had beautiful examples of balanced value levels. My grandparents loved each other, valued their time with one another. It was visibly evident for all to see where their importance levels were. I will never forget the time spent at their feet growing and learning of life's truths directly from their example. They taught me of the Lord and how to have a relationship with Him so that all my other relationships could flourish. They taught me how to love people and focus my love on the Lord first and then my family next before anything else. (I must add a personal note here due to my kids reading this too. I did not always get this right 100 percent of the time. However, in my heart, it has always been a motivating factor of importance for me to strive to grow and develop.)

I had experienced times in my life when I allowed the hustle and bustle of business to take my focus from my family. I had a season in my life with a prestigious job and enjoyed the financial benefits of working hard. There were times during that season of my life when I allowed the draw of finical increase to drive the focus of my value levels. Often the job required me to work late with long commutes, which led to coming home late in the day already exhausted. I would sometimes walk through the door after sitting in traffic, and I would already be ready to go to bed. When the truth is, my family needed me to walk through the door, happy to see them and ready to engage in family community. This time of the day was when we would share how our days went and who needed what, and dinner was made, served, and cleaned up...and then on to a hundred other tasks to complete before bed to prepare for the next day.

When I look back at those days, I realized much of it I was just walking through in a tired daze. I can honestly say that I did not enjoy them as I should have. Now don't get me wrong, there were times of dancing in the kitchen, and water gun fights through the house and singing (we had lots and lots of singing in our home). We have a good family with great memories, but a lot of those days were a blur of what do I have to do next. Now that my children are all grown and have lives of their own. I regret I didn't treasure the moments of that time more.

Who or what holds more importance than your partner in this life? Are you truly partners? Are you in this life battling together against the world or against one another? What is on your priority list before them? Is it time to re-evaluate the value levels you place on your priority list?

Through this coronavirus epidemic with these stay-at-home orders, I have firsthand seen the world come to a screeching halt. Our fast-paced world has now stopped for a moment in time. This pause of life has been eye-opening, to say the least. I pray for all those that are grieving and have lost someone they love in this pandemic. But in my household is has brought enlightenment. I realized how very well I picked my spouse and partner in life. We have been on "stay at home orders" for months now. We have not been anywhere but the grocery store once.

To me, it feels like the last few months have only been a week or two. We have enjoyed our time together, playing card games, doing puzzles, home cooking, and training our puppy together. We have been married for twenty years and enjoy one another's company. However, every time we turn on the television or social media, there are stories of spouses wanting to choke each other and jokes upon jokes about families not getting along and arguing with one another with the feelings of being trapped.

Last night on a news-type talk show, the person interviewed made a comment about being home with the kids and how their family is doing with this electronic home school takeover that has been mandated throughout our country. This reporter said this is the way we put prayer back into school, teach real history and the word of God. The theme of the year 2020 has been staying home with your family and social distancing from everyone else.

The Lord found a way to slow us down and remind us of what is profoundly important. The Lord is giving us time to re-evaluate our relationships, life focuses, and daily routines. All the things that have been waiting until we have time have suddenly found their moment. Today we have nothing but time. Is there any better opportunity to reorganize the priorities in your life?

My prayers and hopes from this pandemic are when it is all over we come out the other side with a better understanding of what is most important. We must remember all we have been given and treasure those special people in our life. We must be sure we are keeping our primary focus on the Lord and then our families before work or volunteerism. Labor should not come before a relationship in a balanced life. Please note, labor should be included in the proper levels. The word of God says if you can work and you do not, you do not eat.

> "For even when we were with you, we gave
> you this rule: 'The one who is unwilling
> to work shall not eat'" (2 Thessalonians
> 3:10, NIV).

Work is important but in a balanced manner rather than a workaholic level. I was taught it this way. In all things, strive for balance and the right order. When you function with your value levels in the order of God, then family (which means spouse, then kids, then the rest of family), then your job (job includes ministry and volunteering, as well as paid employment), then you operate within a healthy balance. Most of the people I see in the counseling office explain feeling major life regrets for the times in life when they had this principle out of order.

An especially important concept to understand is making consistent successful connections and how they work. Every day there are several opportunities for us to make connections with our partner. These connections are attempts to open our thoughts, feelings, and interests to our partner with hopes of a successful connection. The problem comes when we do not understand that these daily life moments are opportunities to bring us closer and closer together.

The important thing to remember is that these moments of connection offer two opportunities: either we are connecting or rejecting one another. If we are not successfully making these connections, then we are rejecting that opportunity. This moment of rejection can often feel like a personal rejection. These may be ridiculously small connections or rejections. However, several small rejections add up one on top of another and can be the driving force to a major disconnect in your relationship. Rejection, no matter how small, still processes as a rejection.

Each of these connection opportunities is like your partner is opening the door to their house (their inner self-thoughts, heart, or mind). They open the door with a simple statement or conversation. If you disregard it as trivial or nonmeaning and choose not to enter in, then it is processed as a rejection. After multitudes of small rejections or misfires, this can build up into bitterness, dissention and can begin to break down the unity of your marriage. If it is not "you and me against the world," then your partner may begin to feel isolated and alone as if it is "me against you and the world."

A simple to understand example is your partner comes to you and shares an idea they have for the weekend. And at that moment, you are tired or busy and respond with "can we talk about this later" or "I don't have time for that now." Within seconds, without even realizing it, this opportunity for connection is rejected. This rejected connection is processed as a misconnect.

This simple choice to give your time and attention to another matter will then be added to the other misconnect rejections instead of a positive connection. I recommend to my counselees, at every opportunity available, stop what you are doing and take a moment to connect. Sometimes this connection only takes a minute, and other times, it may be longer.

Even a small quick connection is better than a rejection. Even by taking time to listen to their idea, then agree to talk about it that evening or the next day will process as a connection. This is because you took the time to show your partner they are important to you, and you care about their thoughts and feelings. These are the best connections because then your partner processes in their minds how important they are to you because you choose to stop what you are doing for their needs and ideas. What a great way to show your priorities and the value you place in your spouse's thoughts and feelings.

These moments of connection can be large and/or small. I have noticed couples seem to do better at understanding the connection or rejection concept when it concerns big issues in your marriage, such as sex, children, and finances. We must also understand, these connections and rejections are important when discussing seemingly trivial topics. Even something as simple as your partner asking you what you want for dinner and responding with you do not care. This response can be processed as a rejection. Can you see how many times in our marriages we are rejecting one another without even being aware of it? I have found increased healing and closeness when both partners become sensitive to the connection opportunities offered by their partner.

There is a secondary method that often is translated into rejection, most often by women (but not exclusively to women). Men tend to listen to others and process to find solutions to issues. Men are wired to find the "fix" to the problems of our world. Women often need to talk and vent their frustrations and feelings. Most of the time, if women are given the opportunity to vent, they will find their own answers in the opportunity of talking it out.

This can be confusing to men; they hear a problem, and their minds somewhat automatically start seeking a solution. This difference in communication is often processed as a disconnect or rejection. If your spouse comes to you and shares with you the stress that is on their mind, and then you proceed to find the solution to fix this problem they are experiencing, this often doesn't feel like you are truly listening to them. You love them and do not want to see them in conflict or stress, so you try to fix it. The problem with this type of reasoning is you do not emotionally enter the situation with them, so they still feel isolated and alone. Once I was working with a couple that was recovering from trauma. The wife was readily trying to share with her husband how she was feeling. He was quick to tell her that the feelings she was feeling were not true and then launched into this is how you fix that problem mode and lecture. When I asked her how she felt once he was done voicing the intelligent ways to solve her problems, she quickly responded that she felt very alone.

I recommended for him to put his personal feelings and problem-solving abilities aside for a moment. I like to ask if we can park that in the parking lot for a moment, and we will come back to it. Once he stopped operating in fix-it mode, he started to hear her pain and confusion. When he really began to listen, they were able to move forward. We then began working towards validation techniques. He learned to tell his wife it made sense she felt the way she does. Her entire countenance changed. I again asked her how she felt, and she quickly said excepted. He held her as she spoke and cried and offered her comfort and validation. This simple change in their personal communication style brought so much healing to their marriage. Sometimes people just need to be heard rather than fixed.

The other factor we must look at is the importance of being physically close, if possible, during these encounter times. In my years of counseling, I have noticed most women prefer some type of touching during these exercises like hand-holding or cuddling, whereas most men prefer for their wives to sit or stand close by them with less touching, especially if they are feeling angry. This is just a personal observation from my counseling office over the years. All men and women are different, so it is perfectly okay if you express differently.

I highly recommend for you to be vocal, tell your partner what you need. The love languages come into play in these times as well. If you have not yet read *The Five Love Languages* by Gary Chapman, I highly recommend it. It is an excellent book with invaluable information on how to give and receive love. I use this tool often in marriage counseling.

If we train ourselves to be more aware of these connections or encounter opportunities and do our best not to miss the chance to love and validate our spouse, it is reciprocated most of the time. If done consistently and correctly, in most cases, this love and validation begins to be exchanged and will flow both ways from one spouse to another.

The Devil in the Details

"Be kind to one another, tenderhearted,
forgiving one another, as God in Christ
forgave you" (Ephesians 4:32, NIV).

The next key factor is not to argue over the details. In my experience, couples can argue or disagree at length over the smallest facts. I have seen this occur about a time or date or what words were exactly said or repeated. The fact does not always matter more than feeling. In the counseling office, we often focus more on how an event or situation made the person feel than the small details found in the factual recall. The trauma or hurt comes from how they feel, and until that feeling is validated and addressed, they generally do not move beyond that pain. When proceeding forward with your spouse, try to concentrate on how they are feeling more so than what you know to be fact.

I cannot tell you how many couples have sat on the counseling couch and argued about the exact words said. As the counselor, I do not care who is right about the exact recall of how something was said. I do care about how each party feels and how to help them move past the feelings of hurt and pain to recovery. Some people have excellent recall, and they remember exact words said. Others try to relate the main point to what was said or done more than the exact word recall. Please note these are two different types of memory recall. Neither one is better than the other. It is simply different people thinking differently, not one person being right and the other being wrong. These small differences in how we process or recall life memories can cause repeated stress and miscommunication.

Many needless arguments have ensued about the factual details; make the conscious choice not to fall into this trap. The moment you stop focusing on the exact factual way an event happened and instead choose to listen to how your spouse feels about the event, you begin to make a powerful connection and move towards resolution and understanding one another. Your relationship will greatly benefit from both of you refusing to argue about small factual details instead choosing to focus on understanding one another's feelings in the situation. Sometimes the most important thing is not who is statistically right, but rather how hurt your partner is by what is happening. When you practice trying to understand how your partner feels, you make them more important than being right about the details. This brings healing to your relationship on a larger magnitude than you may believe.

Fundamentally, we all want to be understood and valued. When your partner sees you valuing their thoughts and feelings beyond your point of view, there is generally a positive connection made. These types of value connections can promote a great amount of openness and willingness to work together. This is a wonderful place to start your journey to healthier habits for your marriage. Begin now by listening to how your spouse communicates their needs and feelings.

These techniques sound simplistic, but they are often awkward in the beginning when you are breaking old bad patterns. Replacing poor strategies for positive ones can feel like work and seem unnatural at first. I encourage you to grow beyond this point. Do not allow yourself to get stuck because it does not feel natural. If you stay with it and be consistent, then the positive behavior will soon feel natural to you. I have heard numerous times in the counseling office that a technique does not feel natural, so people stop utilizing it.

Please understand, this is no reason to stop trying. Not every healthy habit feels natural when you begin to apply it to your life. Just because something feels natural does not mean it is good for you. Often things that do not flow smoothly at first are the greatest skills you can obtain. The equipment you find at the gym screams the truth of this statement.

Every machine in the gym feels like a torture device when you first start to use them. But with perseverance, this can change. The first time I used the stair climber, it wore me out quickly, and I couldn't walk without pain for days. However, after a month or two of consistent use, I found myself building strength and endurance. This machine, in time, became my favorite item to utilize at the gym. A few years ago, it prepared me for a fantastic trip with lots of walking across Israel. Had I not utilized this new technique or equipment in my life, I would have never made it trekking around the desert and mountains. This could not have happened without perseverance and consistency on my part. My hopes are this will encourage you to begin again, to try again, to utilize these techniques consistently to increase the positive value connections in your relationship.

This is the same principle when someone tries to stop cussing and chooses to speak with intelligent words instead. Soon the result of a word fast will change your way of processing your speech patterns. This is training the mind to speak differently and in a more positive and intelligent manner.

This may be difficult at first, but as you practice, it becomes easier and easier. Take the time to listen and validate how your spouse feels about the event or memory you discuss. There is so much to be learned about one another when we understand how the other person feels, rather than arguing about who can recall the facts of a situation more accurately.

LOVE AND FORGIVENESS

The next key factor to cover is the power twins of love and forgiveness. My grandmother taught me when I was small about the power twins. It amazed me because my mother and aunt were twins. All things about twins caught my interest. My grandmother said the power of life is in love and forgiveness. She said with the two twins leading, you were bound to have a successful life full of flourishing relationships. She often spoke to me about forgiveness being the doorway to happiness. As I have matured, I have found her words to be solid truth. The power Twins are the two most essential life truths you will consistently need.

> Dear friends, let us love one another, for love comes from God. Everyone who loves has been born of God and knows God. Whoever does not love does not know God, because God is love.
>
> 1 John 4:7-8 (NIV)

> "And be ye kind one to another, tender-hearted, forgiving one another, even as God for Christ's sake hath forgiven you" (Ephesians 4:32, KJV).

> Judge not, that ye be not judged. For
> with what judgment ye judge, ye shall be
> judged: and with what measure ye mete,
> it shall be measured to you again. And
> why beholdest thou the mote that is in
> thy brother's eye, but considerest not
> the beam that is in thine own eye? Or
> how wilt thou say to thy brother, let me
> pull out the mote out of thine eye; and
> behold, a beam *is* in thine own eye?
>
> Matthew 7:1-4 (KJV)

There isn't a person on the planet that doesn't need for-giveness and love. We often require forgiveness from others for ourselves. We then, too, must apply heaping portions of forgiveness to our partner when they make mistakes. In mar-riage, both you and your spouse will make mistakes and need the healing of forgiveness to be applied. Without forgiveness, none of our marriages can survive. It is not a matter of need-ing forgiveness *if* I make a mistake but more so *when* I make a mistake. We will all take a turn at being at fault at some point in this life together. There was only one perfect person that walked this earth, and that was Jesus. All the rest of us need forgiveness often.

Years ago, an incredibly wise woman taught me a valu-able life lesson. This lesson remains with me to this day. She said choosing not to forgive someone is like you drinking poison, expecting the one that hurt you to die. The poi-son doesn't hurt them. It hurts you. When you are walking through life wounded and hurt, often your pain has extraor-dinarily little effect on the people who hurt you. You become tortured by your inability to forgive those that hurt you. Forgiveness is for your freedom, not theirs.

Forgiveness does not condone what was done to you. Forgiveness frees you from experiencing the pain repeatedly. When you choose the path of not forgiving, it is as if you strap the person that hurt you to your back and carry them around everywhere with you; this sounds exhausting. You are carrying all the weight of what happened, and it may or may not have any residual effect on them. You are carrying around baggage you are not designed to carry. Unforgiveness, when watered with time, will grow into bitterness and resentment. These are hard traits to recover from, and they generally blossom into much larger problems in your relationship and life. Releasing the unforgiveness, choosing to forgive past hurts and offenses sets you free and clears your heart and mind to receive new positive connections. Isn't forgiveness and love better options rather than growing and harvesting bitterness and resentment?

> I want to know Christ-yes, to know the power of his resurrection and participation in his sufferings, becoming like him in his death, and so, somehow, attaining to the resurrection from the dead. Not that I have already obtained all this, or have already arrived at my goal, but I press on to take hold of that for which Christ Jesus took hold of me. Brothers and sisters, I do not consider myself yet to have taken hold of it. But one thing I do: Forgetting what is behind and straining toward what is ahead, I press on toward the goal to win the prize for which God has called me heavenward in Christ Jesus.
> Philippians 3: 10-14 (NIV)

Forgiveness is a choice, and often this can be a difficult choice and an ongoing one. I have often had moments of hurt from another person that I had to forgive them daily until I could finally release the pain and stress caused by the situation. My chosen coping skill in these moments is to release it to the Lord every day and then give *Him* permission to take the unforgiveness from my heart and replace it with *His* forgiveness, love, and peace. When it is too large of a hurt for us to forgive, we can rely on the power of the Lord's love for us as well as the love He has for the one that hurt us.

The Lord loves us all and wants us to be kind and loving towards one another. So, when it is too big for me or you to forgive, please remember nothing is too big for Him. Ask Him to fill your heart with love and forgiveness for the other person and watch as your heart becomes free to forgive. This has been 100 percent successful in my life. There has never been an incident in my life that this method did not work. It wasn't overnight relief most of the time. But with consistency, forgiveness grew, and freedom from the hurt was experienced.

In my personal experiences, I have often found praying for the person who hurt you helps the forgiveness to flow. This is a hard thing to do when the tears are falling from your eyes with pain. Forgiveness is not easy, but it is vital to a healthy life. Ask the Lord to bless the one that hurt you and help them to develop a relationship with Him and allow His love to flow through them. Keep praying every day until you mean what you are praying. No matter how long it takes, stay with it until you mean it.

Once I had a pastor that recommended visualizing a conveyer belt from you to the Lord in heaven. You can place all your worries, frustration, and unforgiveness onto the conveyer belt and send it directly to *Him* to sort out. The moment you put it on the conveyer belt, you agree to let it go and release it to *Him*. Each time you try to take the worry, a thought, or unforgiveness back, you faithfully return it to *Him* on the conveyor belt. You keep repeating this process day after day until you find freedom from the thoughts and feelings. Again, I will stress these methods work if you will do them consistently and intentionally.

How many times should I forgive someone?

> Peter asked Jesus, "How many times should I forgive someone, as many as seven times?" Jesus replied with, "No, you should forgive seventy times seven" (Matthew 18:21, NIV).

Jesus was asked how many times we are to forgive someone that hurts us, and he said seventy times seven. He was telling us to keep forgiving and not give up. Looking at this from the view of you forgiving someone else, this seems ruthlessly unfair to go through this much. But when we discuss this scripture being applied to your own mistakes and misjudgments, it seems almost fair and just for you to be forgiven this much. We want others to forgive us 70*7, but we don't like the sound of having to offer this much forgiveness to those that hurt our hearts. The truth is we are all less than perfect. We often make mistakes that hurt others. The healthiest people are the ones that learn to let go of offenses quickly and completely.

The quicker you let go, the easier it is to release the unforgiveness. The longer you hold on to something, the harder it is to heal from it. This is the perfect point to say if you are holding on to old pains and you have tried everything listed above and still cannot forgive the person that hurt you, please make an appointment with a counselor or pastor and ask for help. Do not let this pain rob you of a healthy and complete life. Seek help and find freedom from these old hurts.

Unforgiveness is a trap that robs people of peace and joy. Unforgiveness can separate you so far from the Lord that you don't know who you are in Him. Unforgiveness is at the root of so much bitterness in relationships and families. The saddest part of that statement is we are in control, and if we would just choose to forgive and love, then healing would follow. If you find this chapter really speaks to you and you have been holding onto unforgiveness, I urge you to pray. Seek the Lord and ask Him to forgive you holding on to unforgiveness. Tell Him you release it all to Him out of obedience to His word and cry out to Him to purify your heart and empty it of unforgiveness and fill it with His forgiveness and love. Repeat this until you find release.

Remember, there is no shame in asking for help when you need it. Find a good godly counselor and work through your stumbling points so you can be free to be all you were designed to be. This freedom also allows you to love the way you were designed to love without holding back due to former hurts. It frees you to walk in good health with all your current and future relationships. I had a pastor who always said if you don't heal the pains of the past, you will bleed on the people who took no part in cutting you. This is valuable advice. Heal from the pains of yesterday so those you love today aren't hurt by your wounds and triggers that they did not cause.

FOCUS ON THE GOOD

The next key factor is focusing your thoughts on what is good about your marriage rather than what isn't going right.

> Whatever is true, whatever is honor-able, whatever is just, whatever is pure, whatever is lovely, whatever is commend-able, if there is ANY excellence, if there is ANYTHING worthy of praise, think about these things.
>
> Philippians 4:19 (NIV)

This scripture teaches us to focus on the positive things in our life rather than the negative. If we learn to apply this scripture to how we view our spouse and relationship, it can turn our mindset into a positive viewpoint.

Not one of us is perfect, not even those who look as if they live the perfect life. However, if we look for the best in others rather than the worst, then we become happier people. When we look for things we think are right in our spouse, rather than seeing (and pointing out) all the things that are wrong with them, we choose to focus on what is uplifting to our marriage.

They say love is blind. I challenge you to remain blind to the minute flaws in your partner and focus your direction of controlled and often redirected thoughts to what you do like, enjoy or appreciate in your spouse. This is a life-changing scripture, memorize and repeat it as often as you need to until it becomes a habit in your life.

A simple technique is choosing to control our thoughts to focus on positive rather than negativity can enlighten your marriage more than you realize. You can also apply these techniques to your children, friends, and co-workers. This one simple biblical principle can be life-changing. Instead of focusing on all the negativity surrounding you, chose to focus on the positive and all that blesses your life. I challenge you to focus the next seven days on teaching yourself to see all that is good in your spouse. Teach yourself to focus on all that uplifts your spouse. Learn to speak to them from the part of your heart that you are training to see the good. It takes time to redirect your thoughts to positivity if you were not born an optimist. However, it is only a matter of teaching and practice to master this art. My beliefs are that once mastered, this technique can enhance relationships within marriage, the family, at work, and with friends.

Some people can automatically see what is wrong with a situation or person but can find great challenges in seeing the positive in the situation. My suggestion is for you to turn this around, choose to see the greatness in those you know and love. It is easiest to learn this technique when you practice on someone you love. Decide to turn off the default of negativity and reset your thinking to seeking out all the good things the Lord has placed in your spouse. When I learned to apply this philosophy to my own relationship, I began to focus on the greatness placed in my husband by our heavenly Father just for our family and me. This one simple daily choice stirs up the love in my heart for my husband instead of stewing up aggravation. It is a simple choice I must make daily. This is not a pass or fail test, but it is one we take daily over and over; some days, this occurs multiple times.

Years ago, I went to a lady's conference where the main theme of the conference weekend was "Garbage in, garbage out." This is a remarkably simple strategy that means what you put into your mind and body is a determining factor as to what will come out of you. There were excellent preaching and teaching on the ramifications of negative thinking and speaking. Then we were challenged to fast complaining for seven days, verbally and in our thoughts. When negativity came to our thoughts, we were taught to cast it down and then change our thoughts to something more positive. After the first seven-day fast, we were challenged to apply it to a specific person or group of people in our lives. Redirecting negative thoughts can be so difficult in the beginning, but once you get focused, it really does bring beauty to your life. I was amazed at the difference in my attitude with these simple changes. I realized quickly how redirecting negativity to thanksgiving can change every day of your life.

I tried these techniques on my husband as soon as I got home. At the beginning of this process, it was a bit frustrating, as I failed almost every other time I tried it. But persistence paid off, and I stuck with it. I found myself falling deeper in love with my husband all over again. This brought my husband and me closer and closer together. He really enjoyed me looking for the best in him, and his self-confidence soared, and he became my Mr. Wonderful once again. Please note my husband did not change; the only thing that changed was my viewpoint of my husband. I changed my life by letting go of negative thoughts, anger from the past, aggravation of daily living and instead choose to look for all that was lovely and pure and good within him and our relationship. I choose to see the good instead of focusing on human flaws.

Seeing firsthand what this did for my marriage, I could not wait to introduce it in the counseling office. This is a technique I share in almost every marital therapy I do. I have firsthand seen this one simple principle help couples fall back in love with each other if done consistently. *Consistency* is a key factor. Commit to doing it and do it! No one is perfect, and sometimes I find myself slipping into old negative thought patterns, but as soon as I catch it, I immediately refocus my attention to the positive. I openly admit I am a work in progress and not perfect. We all are works in progress, so let's agree to be patient with our spouses and ourselves.

We must allow for a growing curve when learning how to apply these new techniques to our lives. It never ceases to amaze me that negativity can reproduce itself so very quickly and easily. However, positivity must be grown and harvested within our lives on purpose with diligent consistency. This makes it imperative that we listen to and self-evaluate our thought patterns consistently to determine if they are based on positive or negative thoughts. The moment we realize we are processing life events through negative vision, we must consciously, on purpose, choose to turn our thoughts to whatever is lovely, good, and pure. This is what the Bible means in the scripture:

> "We destroy arguments and every lofty
> opinion raised against the knowledge of
> God, and take every thought captive to
> obey Christ" (2 Corinthians 10:5, ESV).

I will openly admit it takes some practice and redirection in the beginning to focus on the good instead of the bad, but once you begin, it does get easier. We have been functioning so long in this way. There are times when the negativity never even crosses my mind anymore. This is because I have made it a habit to look for all the good in my husband (and there is so much good there). It started out as me setting my intentions to follow the word of God, and now it is a normal daily function within our marriage. I give the glory to God for showing me this simple principle to keeping the love alive in our marriage.

We are evenly yoked. This means we have the same common core values, ethics, and goals. We are working together to serve our Lord. We have the same beliefs, and this is a common ground of unity in our marriage. This keeps our minds and behaviors focused on the same common direction.

Sewing and Reaping

> Whoever sows sparingly will also reap sparingly, and whoever sows generously will also reap generously. Each of you should give what you have decided in your heart to give, not reluctantly or under compulsion, for God loves a cheerful giver. And God can bless you abundantly, so that in all things at all times, having all that you need, you will abound in every good work.
>
> 2 Corinthians 9:6-8 6 (NIV)

When we apply the concept of sowing and reaping to our marriages, you can better understand the importance of what we put into our marriages. What are you planting into your life together? There are multiple ways to plant. The words you speak, the music you sing along to, the books, movies, and books you view, think earnestly about what you are planting in your mind. This is including the TV shows you watch, magazines, content on your phone, tablet, and computer.

I was told early on in my walk with Jesus if you clean your house, God will bless you. Your house is the physical structure you live within, but this is also applicable to your body and mind as well. The conference mentioned in the last chapter spoke about the garbage we put into our mind and body will then produce garbage out of us. This can be your thoughts, words, and actions. So then protecting what we view, hear, and speak is a vital part of a successful life. One thing can lead to another quickly, and sometimes this happens before you become aware of it.

The safest method is to protect the gates of your thoughts; they are your ears, eyes, and mouth gates. Your ear gates need to be protected from what you are listening to: music, lude jokes, gossip, slander, profane language, these are just to name a few. Your eye gates should be protected from pornography, violent content, crude videos online, and reading things not pleasing to God (yes, ladies, this includes sex/romance novels with sexual content).

Your mouth gates should be protected from all the leaves through your voice: everything you say, whisper or sing. Do you know how important your words are? You could bring blessings or curses into your life by the words you speak from your mouth.

> "The tongue can bring death or life; those who love to talk will reap the consequences" (Proverbs 18:21, NLT).

This is a profound truth most people do not understand. However, once the concept is mastered and you become in control of all the words you speak, it is life-changing. I live by the concept of speaking aloud what you want to manifest in your life until you see it or achieve it. Then quickly thank the Lord for His wonder-working power in your life. When you speak over yourself or your spouse, try to speak affirming words. Let positive intentions flow from your lips. Intentionally choose to speak words that lift you and others rather than tearing down with negative statements.

The second important part of reaping and sowing takes this concept one level deeper. It is important to take a long look at where you are sowing your time and thoughts in your life. I remember when I was a child, my grandfather taught me a valuable lesson.

I was helping him in his garden, watching as he plowed the ground and was readying the ground to plant the seeds he would one day harvest. He showed me the correct way to plant them so they would grow to be healthy mature plants. Then he looked at me and asked me why we were not planting our seeds in his neighbor's yard? I said because these are for your garden. He said yes, it was important that we planted these valuable seeds in his garden so he could harvest them and eat the fruit of his labor. He said the same thing is true in our lives. We must plant the seed of kindness, love, and mercy in our own gardens so we can reap the fruits of our labor in our own lives. He told me we generally plant our seeds in the places that are most important to us. He went on to say some people love their families the most. Some love their jobs the most, some love God and church the most. Regardless of where it is, humans usually plant where they love the most. These words have never left my heart; I understand them clearly today, even if I did not back then.

> Lay not up for yourselves treasures upon earth, where moth and rust doth corrupt, and where thieves break through and steal: But lay up for yourselves treasures in heaven, where neither moth nor rust doth corrupt, and where thieves do not break through nor steal: For where your treasure is, there will your heart be also.
> Mathew 6: 19-21 (NIV)

I have found where your passion is, so will be your time, money, and interest be as well. A workaholic worships their job. An addict worships their next high. A materialistic person's passion is tied up in what they purchase or own. We must look at where we are planting our time, effort, energy, and passions because this shows you what your priorities are in your life. I have seen so many couples in the counseling office, sharing feelings as though their love has mysteriously disappeared.

When we looked deeper at the marriage, we found one spouse was sowing all their time and energy into the kids while the other spouse sowed all their passion for work and hobbies. Neither person was making the marriage a top priority and sowing enough of their seed into their marriage. We cannot give our spouse the leftovers of our day and expect it to create an atmosphere of love and passion. Passion breeds passion, while leftovers tend to breed the feelings of being last on your partner's list.

I heard a pastor say he can take one look at someone's checkbook and tell what they are passionate about because people put their money into what they find important. I will take this one step further and say where your time is. There is where your passion is as well. It just doesn't make sense to me how many people have been in my office desperate to save their marriage, and then I find out they are spending most of their time at work and on their hobbies but pouring very little time and energy into connecting with their partner.

If this hits home for you, then I ask you to re-evaluate your time, effort, and energy and determine how you can shift your focus to your marriage. Rather than watching sports with your friends or going to another get together with friends, maybe your marriage would benefit from a good old-fashioned date night. It is so important to have time for the two of you to show each other how invested you are in making your marriage thrive. Show your spouse they are more important than anything else on your to-do list.

I completely understand that for most people, work is a necessity, not a luxury. However, do you invest most of your time, energy, and passion in your job? I want to warn you this is a mistake. A few weeks after you leave your place of employment, they will have you replaced with someone new. A year after you leave, they may not even remember your name. But your family, that is a different story. They need you and want you to be invested in them.

Your family will never forget you, and your spouse will always need your time and attention. I have left two very lucrative positions for the benefit of my family. My resignation equated to lower-income and our family pinching a few pennies. This decision also led to a much healthier marriage, and our family benefitted in numerous ways. I will never forget my husband's face when I said I was ready to leave these jobs due to them sucking all my time and passion out of me. I explained that I wanted to be more available and tuned in to him and our kids. I do not regret leaving these jobs; the only regret is not doing it sooner. Our family flourished because I made them more important than finances and employment. The word of God says in Mathew 6:21 (ESV):

> For where your treasure is, there your heart will be also". Pay close attention to what you are making your treasure; do not give your heart to things of this world save it for your Lord, your family and those things that are worthy of being your treasure.

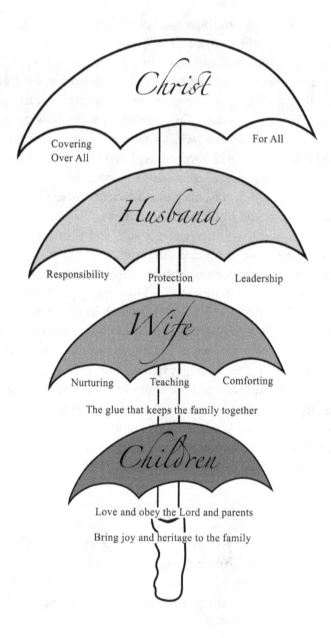

This seems to be the right moment to discuss the hierarchy of the importance of time in a well-balanced life. I was taught a balanced life has priorities in the correct order: God, then family, then our job. What must come first and foremost in our lives is our personal relationship with our Father in heaven above. This is not the ministry you are involved in (that falls under the job category). First on the list is your time spent with God in prayer, fasting, reading your word, personal worship; this encompasses your alone time and personal relationship with *Him*.

The next in line is your family, which breaks down to spouse, then children, then external family and friends that feel like family. Please do not put your children before your spouse. One day (sooner than you know), your children will grow and spread their wings and go create families of their own. If you keep your spouse first on your list when the kids leave home, you two will be able to enjoy your later years together in love as best friends.

When your children are babies, there will be times their needs must come first, but as they grow and become children, your spouse must be before them on the list of your priorities. I have seen so many women get this wrong by making their children their best friends. There is no need to neglect your spouse due to having children in the home. When your children see you modeling healthy behaviors of your spouse being put first (after the relationship with the Lord), they will grow up and find a spouse that will make them a priority as well.

I have seen many marriages go through severe difficulty due to having this God—Family—Job hierarchy wrong. I know how busy life can get with chores, daily to-dos, kids, homework, cooking, cleaning, the list goes on and on. These are all normal parts of daily life we must learn to balance with work responsibilities as well. The problems arise when your spouse loses their correct place on your priority list. Your spouse should be your partner in this life, your best friend that is in it with you. They should be a closer friend than any co-worker, friend, or relative you have in your circle of influence.

When life sends an emergency or illness, this balance can get rocked. It is normal to have a season such as this that can temporarily change your priority list. Good relational health will always come from returning your priorities back to God—Family—Job (in that order) as soon as possible.

Please understand if you are on the church board, or women's ministry, or praise team, whatever it is you do at your church, this is not meant to be placed as the number one priority on your list. Number one is your personal relationship and time with the Lord. Number three is your job. This includes your paid and unpaid positions.

Your volunteer position is a part of your work. I have seen Pastors and people serving the Lord get this tangled up in position number one with their personal relationship with the Lord. They work themselves to the bone serving God at their church without saving time, energy, and passion for their marriage and family. This is a huge mistake that is made rather often in work and ministry. The Lord expects us to keep our priorities, talents, time, and passion in order so our relationships are healthy and balanced. Would the Lord want me to give my passion to the church board, go home tired, and have no passion for my spouse and no energy for my children? The Lord guides us to live a life of balance. How would it change your life and marriage if you worked on getting this one factor in order? Remember it is God—Family—then your job and everything else.

It is also vitally important that you sow seeds of friendship into your marriage. Do not let this go because you have been together for long lengths of time. Friendship will not stay healthy due to the length of the relationship. Choose to be on the same side as your partner; choose to be teammates in this life together. Do not align against your spouse with family members or friends. If the world and all of those in it enter your marriage, then it changes the dynamics of support. It is supposed to be you and me against the world. But if we are against each other, then it becomes you against me.

This means there is no alignment, and the partnership will then begin to fail. Let us stop attacking each other and start attacking "it" together. Unify and attack the source of the problems rather than each other. This creates security within your relationship. It is an incredibly good step in the right direction. Partners should be able to depend on one another for protection, understanding, and acceptance.

I often hear spouses complaining to other people about their frustrations within their home. I want to warn you strongly to prevent this whenever possible. Please note there is a time and place to seek wise counsel, but this is done with someone who seeks the best interest of your marriage and can offer good, sound biblical advice. You will never receive good counsel from someone that will jump on the bandwagon with you and join in with the complaining because you were upset. This will not help your marriage. When you are upset, it is best to pray, calm yourself, then talk it out with the person you are upset with. If that doesn't bring resolution, then get wise counsel for help and try to talk it out again. The word gives us clear instructions in the scriptures:

> Moreover if thy brother shall trespass
> against thee, go and tell him his fault
> between thee and him alone: if he shall
> hear thee, thou hast gained thy brother.

> But if he will not hear thee, then take with thee one or two more, that in the mouth of two or three witnesses every word may be established. And if he shall neglect to hear them, tell it unto the church: but if he neglects to hear the church, let him be unto thee as a heathen man and a publican. Verily I say unto you, Whatsoever ye shall bind on earth shall be bound in heaven: and whatsoever ye shall loose on earth shall be loosed in heaven. Again, I say unto you, that if two of you shall agree on earth as touching anything that they shall ask, it shall be done for them of my Father which is in heaven. For where two or three are gathered in my name, there am I in the midst of them.
>
> Mathew 18:15-20 (KJV)

When upset, first cool off, then talk to one another about it. If that doesn't work, seek wise counsel to work it out. Find the right person to help your relationship, not just side with your way of thinking to help you resolve the issue. If you do not have a person in your life that will not take sides, then seek a wise counselor that will be an advocate for your marriage rather than an advocate for you being declared right about your argument.

If the wife gets upset, then vents all her frustrations to someone else and talks terribly about her husband then she destroys her marriage with her own words and actions. The word of God says a wise woman builds but the foolish woman tears down her own house with her own hands. Plant peace in your home daily and allow it to grow continually.

> Every wise woman buildeth her house:
> but the foolish plucketh it down with her
> hands. He that walketh in his uprightness
> feareth the LORD: but he that is perverse
> in his ways despises him. In the mouth of
> the foolish is a rod of pride: but the lips
> of the wise shall preserve them.
>
> Proverbs 14:1 (KJV)

I have also seen people neglect their personal time with the Lord as a number one top priority. This will bring weakness into your life. We gain our wisdom, strength, endurance, kindness, and guidance from the Lord. If you neglect your personal relationship with HIM, you will quickly lose balance in your world.

> So do not worry, saying, "What shall we
> eat?" or "What shall we drink?" or "What
> shall we wear?" For the pagans run after
> all these things, and your heavenly Father
> knows that you need them. But seek first
> his kingdom and his righteousness, and
> all these things will be given to you as
> well.
>
> Matthew 6:31-33, 31 (NIV)

Seek Him first, make your personal relationship with Jesus Christ the most important element of your life, then family, then your job. When you live this as a life rule, you will find great rewards you did not even know were possible. We all have a part of our lives that are made for a personal relationship with the Lord. In my home, we call this our "God spot." You can try to fill your God spot with work, alcohol, drugs, shopping, money, hobbies, or a multitude of other things. However, until you fill your God spot with a personal relationship with the Lord, there will always be a feeling of something missing in your life. This part of our lives is meant for a personal relationship with the Lord, and nothing else will fill this emptiness until you know Him and create a true personal relationship with the Lord. No matter how hard we try, nothing can fill your God spot except for God. When you get this relationship right first, then all your other relationships fall into the right place.

Reciprocity is a keyword in my industry. Everyone wants to know return on their investment; how does all your giving come back to you? Webster's Dictionary defines reciprocity as "a social norm of responding to a positive action with another positive action, rewarding kind actions." This means giving back in kind what you were given. In counseling sessions, I like to refer to it as the kindness circle. You start by giving kindness repeatedly, and then it comes back to you. Someone must start this kindness and keep it going until it becomes contagious.

I remember when my daughter was little and started daycare. They would send her homesick, and we would all take turns sharing the illness from one to another. We were all sick with it at least twice that year. We just kept it going around. How would your home change if kindness and love were as contagious as the flu? Can you be so kind to your partner that they give it back to you?

Once the circle of kindness gets flowing, it generally keeps flowing from one spouse to the other; this is reciprocity at its finest. If I spend the entire week being kind to my husband, it never fails before the week is over, he is telling me, "I like it when you are sweet." He responds to feeling the love by giving me more love. Happy brings happier, and who better to share and practice this on but your spouse? There is no guaranteed turnaround time on the niceness circle, but if at least one of you are trying your best, then there is the hope of positive change in your marriage.

Anger begets resentment that will then grow into bitterness. Bitterness leads to painful disconnection. But kindness begets forgiveness that grows love. Forgiveness is a blooming fruit of love. The atmosphere relationships flourish most within contains large amounts of kindness, love, and forgiveness.

Small, consistent changes can bring you and your spouse closer each day. Intimacy grows because you choose to connect with each other. We have daily choices to connect and grow closer or disconnect by rejecting one another, which leads to growing apart. Little daily rejections can grow into large painful disconnects. Start now, focus your attention and energy on you being kind to your spouse, try to show the love of Christ through all you do and say to one another.

For some people, kindness is an ingrained trait; they smile easily, and they are approachable. There are also those that must learn to be kind, and some that appear to have a do not disturb sign on their forehead. Regardless of whether you were born with kindness, it can be learned. How kind you are is not determined by your upbringing or experiences. Kindness is a choice. You can learn to respond with niceness to your spouse, family, and others in your life. If you have tried and failed in this area, I urge you to try again. If you still feel like something is blocking you, maybe there are deep feelings or pain you need help overcoming. If this describes you, then seek help with a good godly counselor to figure out why and overcome this challenge.

CLEAR COMMUNICATION

The next key factor we must discuss is communication. So often, the biggest problems I see in relationships seeking marital counseling are due to poor communication habits. When communication is poor or nonexistent, trouble is bound to erupt. Marriage counselors often do a lot of interpreting for couples until effective communication is learned and utilized. We all have different communication styles depending on sex, upbringing, historical events, maturity, and culture.

It is normal for our partners not to completely understand everything we say. The irony of this is couples that have been together for long periods of time often expect their partners to completely understand them. They think their partner can read their minds and understand exactly what they have said or how they meant what they said. The truth is no one can read your mind, even if you have been married for a long time. We still must utilize effective communication to prevent misunderstandings. There is a tried-and-true method that has been used in the counseling office for many, many years. Please do not skip this part if you have heard it before. We should all review these techniques often. If this method is utilized, it can prevent hurt feelings, misunderstandings, and arguments. So, it is worth your time to master this technique to enhance your styles and methods for effective communication.

The "process and switch method" begins with your partner sharing what they want to communicate with you. While they are sharing, you listen intently. Listening intently means with your body turned towards your partner, looking at them, and you are silent. During this exercise, remove distractions such as television, computer, or your cell phone. When they finish talking, you repeat back what you think you heard them say. I recommend statements like, "If I understand you correctly, you are trying to say…" or "do I understand you correctly; are you trying to say…"? If your partner says you are wrong and did not understand correctly, then ask them to try to repeat, but this time ask them to use different words. Keep doing this until you have verified you understood their meaning. Then when you reach a complete understanding of your partner, you can switch. Now it is your turn to process and share all your thoughts while your partner listens silently to you until they completely understand your point. This progress may take you more time than your usual conversations, but it guarantees to stop poor communication and replace it with a better understanding of each other's feelings and thoughts. I must stress the importance of no interruptions. "Process and switch" is an effective communication skill used all over the world in counseling offices because it works.

When you communicate effectively by truly listening and understanding one another, it limits your arguments drastically. I have found this method requires more time and self-control; however, it is an effective way to communicate and helps you and your partner focus on listening to understand rather than listening to respond. Most people listen to part of what is being said. Then, their brains automatically begin to think about how they will respond rather than truly listening to understand the other person's thoughts, concepts, and views on the situation and feelings they are experiencing. Especially with women, if you only listen to the beginning of what is said, you miss a good portion of content explaining the feelings behind the thoughts. The differences between men and women communication styles can play a key role. Women generally describe all the details prior to saying the important statements. This means you need to listen until the end to understand what is being said. This can be difficult for men because men generally say the most important facts first in discussions. I have noticed most men listen to the first few sentences their spouse tries to communicate then begin working on solutions in their minds rather than listening to all of the content their wife is trying to relay to them.

As a counselor, I spend a good majority of my time teaching people how to listen. Most people can speak well, but listening is a talent that must be practiced and mastered. This is an even harder skill when it pertains to someone you have known for a long time. We think we know how they will finish their thoughts before they say them. Especially when you already know all the historical stories they routinely tell. It is much easier to listen to someone you just met and are trying to get to know than someone you know very well. It is so important that we master intently listening when our spouse wants to share their thoughts and feelings with us, no matter how long we have been together. Intent listening leads to a connection instead of listening to respond that leads to rejection.

We must also discuss the art of being interested. This is an amazingly easy task when you are dating, and you do not know all their thoughts and opinions yet. However, when you have been together long enough to know what story they are about to tell because you have heard it four hundred times, truly listening is much harder. After being together for a long time, it becomes easier to not truly hear what the other person is saying. Or even worse, guess what they are about to say and begin working on your response before they have even finished speaking. I challenge you to listen to your partner intently even if you have heard the same thing a million times because this time, there might be new information.

But most importantly, it shows your partner you respect him or her enough to give them the gift of your time and full attention. This one simple act can loudly communicate the depth of your concern for your partner and how much you truly value their voice and thoughts. If you want your partner to feel valued, then you must begin to listen to understand instead of listening to respond to them.

Good communication is an art; unfortunately, it is a slowly dying art. People seem to want to be heard more than they want to listen and hear viewpoints that may be different from their own. But this is where we grow when we listen to others with different views on subjects than we do. When we listen to their insight, sometimes it will adapt our way of thinking and methods of responding. This can spur growth and development in our own behavior methods. I long ago had a pastor that would remind us rather often. We have two ears and only one month; because we should *listen* twice as much as we speak. I believe this to be good advice. Try putting it into practice in your life and watch those around you begin to share more of how they think and feel with you.

I once worked at length with a gentleman in this area. We all know people like him; if he was in the room, he did 85 percent of the talking. After much behavioral training, he mastered the art of listening. He came back to see me in the counseling office six months later and reported he was promoted to a higher-level position at work. He also shared his marriage was better than it had ever been, and he had several new remarkably interesting friends.

When he was doing all the talking, he showed others he was not interested in them or what they had to say. Once he began to close his lips and open his ears, and use positive body language while listening, he began to attract people to him rather than pushing them away. His supervisor even began to give him accolades for the improvement of his work. He shared with me that he did not change his work habits, only his listening habits. Listening is an extremely important part of effective communication.

These simple behavior changes can open new relation-ships, begin to repair damaged relationships, and grow your understanding of the needs of those you love. Most people have an inner desire to be heard and understood. Listening in order to understand adds value level to your relationship. It shows your spouse, their thoughts, feelings, and needs are high on your priority list.

I want to encourage you to use these skills even when the topic is heated or appears uninteresting to you. Value your spouse enough to give them your time to truly listen to their feelings and ideas.

One last point on communication that is important to discuss is body language and the tone you speak in. There are many people on the planet that sound aggressive when they do not mean to. I think we can all think of someone in our lives that seem mad even when they aren't. You must be aware of the tone of your voice and body language for clear, effective communication to occur.

Try to be more in touch with how your body language appears and how forceful or sarcastic your tone sounds. Many arguments are started with these two simple factors. Be aware if you sound as though you are upset. Be more in touch with what you are communicating in nonverbal ways. Some people speak loudly with abrupt sounding tone and can communicate they are upset when in fact, they really aren't.

When communicating with your spouse or children, be intentional in your tone and body language. If you are a tall person or have a large stature, then try sitting down to talk to your kids or spouse. If you are normally loud-voiced, try to intentionally lower or calm your tone. Be aware of the stance you are in and what it is communicating to those around you. Try using a gentle tone and body language and see the difference it makes in the way what you say is received by those listening to you.

CAREGIVING

The next topic I want to cover is the art of caregiving. There are some people that are natural-born caregivers. They always just seem to know how to take care of people and what the person they are caring for needs. It is an almost instinctive reaction to a person in need that comes easily without much effort. Generally, these types of people need little training to be exceptional caregivers. I was born with this trait and found it irritating when someone else did not understand what came so easy for me.

I have learned through experience that everyone is not given this as a natural gift. Often, it must be a learned trait. During most wedding vows, we commit to love in sickness and health for a particularly good reason.

If you are not a good caregiver, then learn how to be better. If your partner is down for physical or mental health issues, then you need to step it up and take care of your teammate. There will be times in life when we need some type of loving care from our spouse.

In my personal marriage, we have witnessed everything from flu, surgery, mental breakdown to grief beyond understanding. And in these moments, we stood together and cared for one another. When we were first married, my husband was a great provider and a wonderful friend, but he was not a good caregiver. He was young and had no experience caring for another person. He was used to others caring for him. Life gave us both experiences to grow and mature. I was diagnosed with a terrible disease that would strand me for days in bed in high levels of pain. In was in these years, he learned to be the wonderful caregiver he is now. Caregiving was a learned behavior that he has grown better and better at by practicing. This took a lot of patience on both of our parts.

I never thought I would have the opportunity to say this. Now, when I am ill, if I can choose who takes care of me, I prefer it to be my husband. He now cares for me as good, if not better, than I care for him. So again, if you are not a good caregiver, take the initiative and change this about yourself. Learn to show people how valuable they are by offering loving care when needed.

No matter how difficult the journey, no matter how long the road, we decided whatever life brought our way, we would walk it out together. My husband tells me often that it is him and I against the world. This is one of his favorite sayings because we both fought life's battles alone for many years before we met. The fact we fight all battles together makes us stronger and offers security that someone always has my back in the battles of life.

There are two options, the first being you and me against the world and the second being me against you, and all the world throws at me too. Then it really is me against you, and "it," the "it" can be anything that is attacking your peace. Do not attack your spouse; unify with your spouse so that together you both can fight whatever it is that is coming against you. Strength comes when we are a united front. This is true with everything, from finances to people's problems. This is especially true when the battles are with extended family or even your own children. A marriage can quickly be made weak when an external force invades the unity between a husband and wife. I believe this is one reason the Lord said:

> "Therefore a man shall leave his father
> and his mother and hold fast to his wife,
> and the two shall become one flesh"
> (Matthew 19:5 ESV).

A man will leave his mother and father and cleave to his wife. This means our unity evolves from our original family unit to the new one we create with our spouse. This unity must come first before any other earthly relationship. There will be moments of disagreement about the children or external family, but you must remain a united front and discuss your viewpoints with one another privately until you are able to agree. This deep partnership is not easily broken because it is wrapped in the third strand of our cord. This third strand to the cord is our strength that comes from the Lord holding the right position in our marriage.

I openly admit it takes time to understand when someone is sick or hurt (and to what level) if they are not effective at communicating their own needs. My husband has mastered this art over the last twenty years. He can tell when I am sick before I can. He knows when I am exhausted and has an uncanny way of knowing when I just need to rest. He can read my body language and mannerisms, and he helps me by reminding me to care for myself better. He reminds me if I do not take care of myself, then I cannot help anyone else. He sees things in me that I do not realize in myself. And I offer this same benefit to him. I often can tell when he isn't feeling well by simply paying attention to his expressions. This took time for us to understand each other. When my husband tells me it is time for me to rest, I listen. I know he offers this sound advice for my own protection.

I have come to know what anxiety looks like in my husband's eyes, and when he says nothing is wrong when something is most definitely wrong. I have learned how to gently redirect the subject of the conversation to what he is feeling and why. This is done without pushing but with offering to listen. It is also important to be oh so careful not to miss the opportunity when he opens the door to his feelings. In these moments, we must be highly aware and prevent any rejection of our partner's attempt to share. When he begins to share, I try to stop all distractions and intently listen and validate how he feels. He has repeatedly expressed what a great help this is to him.

I have taken care of my husband after surgery when he was in pain and a difficult patient, and with a glad heart, I can report he took good care of me when I had my surgeries, and I was a difficult patient. He learned a great deal about being the caregiver when I had major surgery several years ago. My surgical recovery turned our lives upside down for a while. He was kind, patient, always by my side, and willing to help whenever I needed it. I can only imagine how hard life would have been without him. I am very thankful for his never-ending support. We have had a lot of ups and downs in this life journey together, but we held on. We held on tight with both hands. We agreed to never let go of each other even when, in moments of hurt or desperation, we wanted to give up. I encourage you to be intent on staying together and holding on to one another, no matter what life sends your way.

There have been times of great sorrow that also become caregiving times. When my mother went to be with Jesus, it was incredibly painful for me. I spent weeks caught in uncontrollable emotions of grief. Then when it seemed like joy was returning to life, we lost ten more friends and relatives over the following year and a half. This included my best friend in this world too. Some of my favorite people are sitting with Jesus in heaven right now. This was a two-year period of compounded grief that turned our world inside out. We both had emotions that were raw and sensitive with noticeably short fuses. There were immense pain and sorrow that our world had never experienced such depths in such a short time. I remember moments thinking I will never be happy again, and my world will never be the same. I was right that my world will never be the same again but terribly wrong that I would never be happy again. I miss all of those I have lost, but I sit here writing this with hope for the future in my heart once again. This is because my husband was there with me, he too felt what I was feeling, and we worked through it together. We talked for hours of all we missed and cherished of those we had lost. During that two-year period, it truly was my husband and I against the world of grief. I say that with the full meaning of the Lord was the third strand to our cord.

> "And though a man might prevail against one who is alone, two will withstand him-a threefold cord is not quickly broken" (Ecclesiastes 4:12 ESV).

A cord with two strands can be broken easily, but the third strand makes it strong enough to withstand so much more pressure. When a husband and wife do not have close relationships with the Lord, they are a two-stranded cord. But when they have the Lord in *His* rightful place, there is a third strand to the cord that makes it exceptionally harder to break.

I added grief to the caregiving part of this book because, to this day, my husband cares for my heart and the pain left from grief. Today is my birthday, and it being right in the middle of the holiday season. I miss my Mom and my best friend more today than usual days. My sweet husband knows this and keeps the viewing on the television light and funny—no shows with death scenes or sadness. He arranges a fun day for me and babies me a little extra, so I feel loved and special. He does the work to bless me, care for me, and give me a special day. This is the epitome of caregiving, seeing your partner in need and providing it for them.

There are some personality types that were created to be caregivers. It is an instinct for them to serve those they love. But there are also personality types that are not natural caregivers. This must be a learned skill for them because it is not instinctual. This often requires patience and good communication for both parties involved. If instinct does not tell you when a person is in need, then verbal communication is the best method to engage for better understanding. If you do not understand what your partner needs, ask them. Keep trying until you can clearly understand. This is one of those areas that practice makes perfect. The more you try, the better you will get at this skill. And, most importantly, when they share how they feel, stop what you are doing and truly listen. Be extra careful there is no rejection in these moments, give them your full attention.

SEX AND INTIMACY

The next key factor worthy of covering is sex and intimacy. Both are key factors for a healthy marriage.

Communication is an important part of all aspects of your relationship; this includes satisfying sex as well. It benefits your marriage when you are kind but honest with your partner about the things you enjoy in sex and those you do not. You should be able to be open and honest with your partner about sex. Share what is enjoyable and what is not. Share your fantasies and desires. Talk with your partner if you feel your needs are not being met. Talk about what does it for you, what you want to try, and what you want to stop doing.

One partner should never push the other into doing things they are not comfortable with; however, you can talk about what you want and what aspect makes them uncomfortable. Share your inner thoughts, feelings, and dreams about sex with your partner. If one is unaware of what the other one genuinely wants, then you run the risk of never meeting each other's needs. I say to you, most hungry men and women will only fast so long before they find somewhere to eat. The same goes for sex. If you are not meeting one another's needs, you may be opening your relationship up to an affair. Protect your marriage by open communication and effective listening, being welcomed even in the area of sexuality, especially in the area of sexuality. It is important to discuss the things you want to try within the boundary of experimentation. Keep the predators of your marriage away by meeting the needs you both have within the marriage.

Long ago, I heard a woman say in a women's conference, "it doesn't matter how old, how young, how thin, how plump, how smart sarcastic your spouse is…if you are tired of your spouse and no longer want them, be aware there is another person who is all alone that would gladly take your spouse". I believe this to be true for men and women. If you do not love your partner to the best of your ability, please know there is someone else out there that would gladly try to take your spouse's love and attention. We must learn when we do not value what we have been given, someone else will. I have seen this time and time again in the counseling office.

The statistics on affairs are mind-blowing. Years ago, you rarely heard of a woman having an affair and leaving her family. From time to time, you did hear of this with men leaving their families for a love affair. But currently, the statistics of a marriage surviving without at least one affair is 35 percent. The statistics show women now cheat just as often as men do. The marital health research network states the percentage of marriages where one or both spouses admit to infidelity, either physical or emotional: 41 percent. Twenty-two percent of men admit to straying at least once while being married. The average length of an extra-marital affair: two years. Could this correlate with how self-focused our culture has become? Could it be we think more about ourselves and our own needs than we do of our partner's needs?

My grandfather lived his life caring for my grandmother first and foremost in all he did. I can say she functioned in the same manner; everything was for him and to meet his needs. They were wise and had an extremely successful marriage because they were always putting the other one first. He had his needs met, and she had hers met. Never self-focused but always spouse-focused. This prevented anyone from coming between them.

In the bible we have the book of the Song of Solomon as an example to a godly intimate relationship. It provides excellent examples of lifting one another up, speaking with love words and enjoying the intimacy that comes from love. If you have yet to do a study on the Song of Solomon, I encourage you to do so with your spouse. The Lord has this book in the bible to show us the appropriate way to love and enjoy our marriages.

I cannot tell you how many couples I have counseled over the years have shared how sexually frustrated they are within their relationship. Sexual frustration can explode or spill over onto all other aspects of our relationship and cause multiple problems. Sexual frustration can begin due to a lack of sex or an unmet sexual desire. It is common for your sexual preferences to differ a little or a lot. The most important factor to couples with satisfying sex lives is they openly communicated wants and needs. This may seem awkward at first if this is not what you are accustomed to, but there should be no sexual topic that can't be discussed privately between you and your spouse. This type of communication is also valuable when sharing with your partner your likes and dislikes. Let me caution you at this point if your partner is doing something you do not enjoy, please use kindness and gentleness when you discuss it. In these discussions, you can build your spouse up or tear them down; this is one of the most sensitive areas. Tread lightly, speak kindly but be honest.

Believe it or not, in long-term relationships, sex has seasons. There are cold seasons like the deep winters up north, but there are also hot seasons like summers down here in the south. These seasons may not fall at the same time as both spouses are different, but often, partners seem to take turns. One partner is hot while the other is not so hot. I have counseled with husbands sharing their unmet needs and wives sharing the same frustrations, both asking for intimacy and neither understanding how to communicate it nor even where to begin to get their needs met. Instead, they both remain frustrated on "their side" of the unmet need. Developing a better understanding through clear communication is the best recommendation in these times. The more the two of you talk about your sex life (successes and unmet needs), the better the chances are of you having enjoyment in your sex life together. But again, I want to stress—do so in a kind manner.

Beware of the spirit of Jezebel, the sneaky one that tries to destroy your marriage. Watch for her trying to sneak her way into your home. Even when you cannot see her, you can feel her. We doubt these feelings and talk ourselves out of them, but we know when evil tries to enter our homes. It is uncanny how many times I have heard during a counseling session, "I just knew something wasn't right," or "I just felt like something was wrong with him or her." Deep inside, we can feel when something is off and should address it as soon as we begin having those feelings.

Back in the olden days, they had a watchman that would stand on top of the protection walls of the city. Their job was to stand guard and watch for threats against the city. They protected everyone in their charge. In fact, if they were not at their stations, then everyone's lives were at stake. Our homes need watchmen on the walls to stand guard against predators of our families. If we are watching, we often can see the trouble before it reaches us. Be aware of the weaknesses within your relationship and do something to strengthen them.

If you are experiencing sexual miscommunication, I urge you to try to work through it together. If you are unable to find a resolution after several tries, I highly recommend you book a few sessions with a good Christian counselor for help. Who is the watchman for your relationship? Are you the watchman? You must take turns to keep your vision clear. Do not become so busy in duties that we neglect the importance of the watchmen of our lives. We must all be watchmen in our marriages and homes. We must be on alert to when something is trying to attack the sanctity of our homes.

Happily married couples are beautiful people. Happiness is attractive. It is a glow that most people can see. When someone is happily in love, they are incredibly beautiful; this holds true for men and women. This also means they become more attractive to others around them.

The rule is, do not look to the left or the right. Always keep your eyes on the three strands of your cord. "You, me, and Jesus" do not allow your eyes to become lustful and look beyond that. Keep your desires focused on your marriage. Do the work, talk it out, work for what you want, and take the time to enjoy the exploration together. When we are focused on protecting each other and meeting one other's needs through the power of love, then this beauty is present for all to see. This is the love that I believe, deep down, we all want and seek.

Do not let your eyes stray, even looking at another person with lust. Most that have fallen to adultery have fallen into this track first with a look. If you are in a committed marriage, I say to you, and rule number one is—*do not look!* Protect your eyes gates. Too much garbage enters through our eyes.

We turn on the TV and let all kinds of garbage into our heads. I saw a burger commercial the other day full-blown soft porn…on TV, where even our children can see it. I quickly said if you need sex to sell your burger, it must be bad, and we turned the station.

The truth is you cannot stand in the checkout line at the grocery store without seeing a pornographic image on a magazine. When our eyes see sex and violence on TV, in movies, and video games, it de-sensitizes our spirits to these things. We can become cold to things that should stir reaction within us.

For example, if pornography is used, we can see how de-sensation can affect an entire marriage through one-party introducing these sexual nuances into the marital home. It is uncanny how often I sit with couples trying to recover from infidelity and find it began with pornography. If the eye gates are opened with porn, then the viewer's brain becomes less sensitive to sexual sight and needs more and more images to become satisfied in sexual encounters, often leading to lower interest in spouse and justification in this process. I hear statements such as "She does not want me anyway," or "I do not get what I need from her."

The best advice I have ever heard on sex is this:

- Wives—If your husband wants to have sex, give him sex. If possible, make it happen as soon as you can.
- Husbands—If your wife wants to have sex, give her sex. If possible, make it happen as soon as you can.

Keep it just that simple and hold to it as often as possible (there are times when it just is not doable—that is completely expectable. Just *do not let it become a rule*). If you are getting your needs met at home, why look for them to be met anywhere else? This rule comes from the Bible. Our bodies are not our own. They belong to our spouse. This is how we are created to go together. If we always protect that, then there is a truly committed bond like none other.

> The husband should fulfill his marital duty to his wife, and likewise the wife to her husband. The wife does not have authority over her own body but yields it to her husband. In the same way, the husband does not have authority over his own body but yields it to his wife. Do not deprive each other except perhaps by mutual consent and for a time, so that you may devote yourselves to prayer. Then come together again so that Satan will not tempt you because of your lack of self-control.
> 1 Corinthians 7:3-5 (NIV)

This scripture means when your spouse needs sex, you make a point to meet that need. I have heard many spouses reporting they will do this, but it is often with a "hurry up and finish" attitude. I want to warn you this will not affair-proof your marriage. Your spouse wants to be desired and wants your full attention and participation. This is a vital part of sexual contentment; this is another area for the two of you to be open and honest and communicate clearly.

All marriages have moments when the sexual desires are almost equal, and then there are times when one party wants or needs more interaction than the other. In my own marriage, there have been seasons where we were both on fire, as well as seasons when only he or only I was on fire with desire. There have been cold seasons as well. We have been very blessed the cold seasons are as short as the winters are here in Florida. I thank God for this and our constant need to care for and love one another. It has also grown with our maturity in life, and it is much easier once all the kids move out of the house and you are not caregiving daily. However, we persevered through those days as well. We even had a hot sex life with teenagers in the house and full-time jobs. Sometimes laundry or dishes had to wait because the last of our energy was spent on pleasing each other. These are words to live by. Is your marriage more important than getting the daily chores completed?

I was raised in a neat freak home, and I was a neat freak myself until the day I realized my husband went without his needs being meet so that I could vacuum the floors. The next day the chores waited, and I pleased my man. And I have tried to honor that way of thinking since then, and he has done the same for me. We live in a clean house but not obsessively clean. It allows me to have time and energy for the love of my life. I had to add energy to this statement because giving your body is not to just lay there and allow them to do what they want. Sex should be an interactive experience. It is a two-person sport; you both need to play. If you are unsure of this fact, again, I say take some time and read the book of Song of Solomon in the Bible. The entire book is of love and cherishing and giving of oneself. We were designed to love. Our bodies perfectly fit together and need each other, just as our Lord designed them.

I recommend you keep your eyes focused on your spouse and their sexual needs and desires, and they keep their eyes on your needs and desires. I recommend you develop an open dialogue sharing with your partner the truth of your wants, wills, and sexual desires. If you don't talk to your partner and share your desires, how will they know? If you don't discuss the things you want to try, how will they know? No matter how long you two have been together, your partner is not a mind reader. The best marriages have great communication skills. Maybe it is time to increase these skills in your own marriage.

Trust and Unity

The next factor we must discuss is vitally important to a successful marriage. All marriages need trust and unity.

Unity is one of the most important factors in marriage. We must be a united front against the forces in the world that would like to destroy our marriages. There should be a natural alliance between you, your spouse, and the Lord. We must work daily to protect our unity bond. When we are in unity (or on the same page), we can stand together no matter what is attacking our relationship. This leads us back to the theory of either it's you and me against the world or you and the world against me.

My husband loves old 1940's movies. We watched one last night, and there was this scene where the commander ordered the soldiers to "form the turtle." Once the leader made the command, the soldiers began to move into a formation that protected them all from the danger of attack. I joked, saying that is the skill we need in the counseling office for the attacks on our families and marriages.

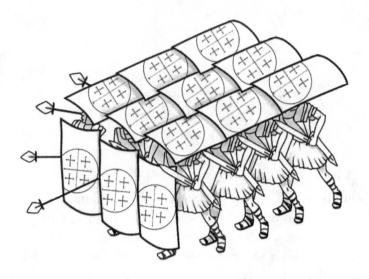

When the Roman Commander would call for his troops to form the turtle (also known as the legendary *testudo formation*), they would gather closely together and raise their shields in unity to encompass all of the soldiers within that unit. Safely covered by the collective shields, they could move forward to attack their enemy in a complete shell of protection for the troops. Each soldier was doing their part to keep the entire unit safe.

There are many times in life when the attacks come against our relationships, and we need to form the turtle to protect our family from the enemy's attack. We must close ranks, hold up our shields and prepare for battle, all while working together in unity to fight our enemy as a team. *We* hold up shields by remaining faithful, covering each other in prayers, working together, and communicating effectively, just to name a few. When our partners hold up their shields, and we hold up ours, together this turtle shield covers us from the fiery darts launched at us. So, the big question becomes, can I trust my spouse to hold up his or her side of the shield to protect us when in turbulent trouble?

Trust needs to be established and protected within the marriage and family. The question of whether to trust or not trust someone that has let you down or hurt you before can be a hard question to answer. Forgiveness is mandatory in the Christian walk; however, trust is not. Trust must be freely given by choice. Once trust is lost, it must be earned back carefully and purposefully. Honesty and transparency are vital tools present in earning trust.

There are two issues with trust I would like to discuss in this chapter. The first being when someone within your inner circle hurts you and the relationship continues, and you must reestablish the trust and connection. The second is when a separate person (often from your past) has hurt you deeply, and you are trying to move forward with the pain from yesterday, and it is now affecting your current relationships. The first is keeping a relationship alive, and the second is cutting an old relationship free from your life.

In my experiences, I have found it much easier to forgive those people that hurt me then left my life. Once they were out of the picture, my hurt feelings cooled off, and I was able to apply the forgiveness principles of the Bible. I find the faster you do this, the easier it is. Make your habit be one of forgiving quickly and letting go of bitterness as fast as you realized its presence in your emotions. I have had close relationships come and go, many leaving painful emotions in their wake of abandonment. These pains must be forgiven for new healthy growth to occur. If you do not forgive those who have hurt you, you will bleed on the next person who enters your life, and they didn't even do anything wrong, other than unknowingly hitting your trigger left by the old pains of yesterday.

When someone mistreats you, and you allow it to change you or prevent you from helping the next person, it not only affects you, but it can affect all of those in your life. Does it make sense for someone else's mistakes or manipulations to cause you to stop believing in or connecting with others? Is it true one bad apple can ruin the whole barrel? So, each time our hearts are hurt, do we lose a little more compassion and openness with one another?

Do the manipulators in this world stop us from loving or helping others? I see this often in the counseling office, and there were times I hate to admit I saw this in myself. My true heart is I wish I had more wisdom and self-control, but heartbreak is always hard to recover from. I'm a sucker for a do-over story. I love to encourage and see others succeed. I am drawn to those who do not give up and try as many times as it takes to succeed. I love to celebrate a survival story. I, myself, have a wonderful survival story in my life. We must celebrate these moments in life because they are the moments that love and forgiveness win over betrayal and pain. Just because we have experiences with manipulators and users does not mean we have to allow them to change our hearts to coldness and bitterness. Instead, we can choose to forgive and love again and continue to give to those that need us the most.

This area requires much wisdom because a user, a taker, a manipulator, can see a giving heart, and they will try to use them for all they can and then quickly move on to the next kind soul. We must use wisdom and discernment as to who we open our hearts to. But there must also be a balance that we don't stop helping others. Even with your best discernment abilities, it's possible to believe in someone and get used in spite of your efforts. Just as a sidebar, this type of person will use you up and then talk bad about you on their way out of the door.

I used to worry people would hear and believe something that was being said about me that wasn't true. This really bugged me, so I went to my pastor and shared my fears. He is a kind and wisdom-filled man. He told me if I defend myself, God won't defend me, but if I need the Lord and ask and let Him defend me, then I will find the victory. He also said live a life so that if anyone talks bad about you, no one will believe it. Again, we are discussing the need for forgiveness in our lives for those that disappoint and hurt us.

There is a point in life where we must lay down those hurts and heavyweights of yesterday so we can be free to live today to its fullness. I have been a part of many people's start over. Some went very well and some not so well. But I am committed to helping people. I will not allow the few bad people to remove the seeds I sow because some of them grow in good soil. If I stop caring, then I am guaranteed to help no one, but if I keep trying, the odds are, I will be able to help somebody. I choose to have an optimistic heart but must stress that it is a choice.

My life has been blessed beyond anything I deserve. If you added up all the tears and hurts or pain, I have been blessed way beyond the pain, even though that's hard to believe. Somewhere, somehow, I believe you will get what you give in this life. Remember the bible scripture we looked at earlier that says you will reap what you sow. Simply put, the seed you plant will grow. I choose to give this world my love and encouragement, and I choose not to allow anyone who tries to use or manipulate me to change that which I can give to those in need.

Can your partner be trusted to hold up their end of the shield? Can you be trusted to hold up your side of the shield as well? This is not to just protect one person in the family but the entire family. We keep each other safe. Our goal is to keep the enemy out of the family unit. We must hold our shields high and hold onto one another through the storms of life. Life is best when we protect, hold on to and forgive one another, make this the collective goal of your family.

I cannot stress unity enough. There is such power when a family comes together in unity. It should be your unity that keeps you focused on the common good of the marriage. It will keep you bound together. Keep your focus on each other; don't let things that glitter draw your attention with distraction. Instead, restore the shine and find the sparkle in your marriage and if it's not there, then work for it until you have it.

I've known so many relationships fail due to boredom at home, and one or the other finds excitement somewhere else. Unfortunately, this happens with wives and husbands equally. Sex and excitement can be found all too easy outside the marriage partnership. The point I am trying to make with this sad fact is for one moment or season of excitement and pleasure, so very much is sacrificed. The sanctity of the marriage is thrown away, all trust is lost, their friendship is greatly damaged. And when children are involved, the pain magnifies. It would take a whole other book to explain the damage it leaves on the children. One person steps outside the marriage to have an affair, but the entire family pays for it. Often, it's the children that pay the most and suffer the deepest wounds to their psyche.

The purity of the marriage bed may sound to you like old-fashioned terms, but I believe this to be a wise goal for happiness and friendship that often outlives the excitement and desires. We should all strive to achieve purity in our marriage beds. This simply means our sex life and the most intimate part of our own emotions are only shared with that one person, our spouse. If at all costs, we refrain from sexual intimacy with others outside the marriage, this purity will help strengthen the friendship and life commitment. This is done by preventing ourselves to bond with another that can take our interest and stir excitement. I offer old-fashioned warnings here, but a lot of the old ways are ways we should instill in our families today. They are so needed today.

I caution married women about having close friendships with other men and married men having close friendships with other women. Be warned, be careful. It's just not a good idea, and it can set up stumbling blocks for a future fall that can be devastating. These situations are best when there's a group friendship you don't bond with one more than anyone else in the group. So many times, I've seen people become "just friends," and then after some time, they start emotionally bonding too much. The bond becomes stronger in an area than what they have with their spouse, and then their intimacy begins to transfer from spouse to this exciting new friend. This can easily lead down a path that can break the purity of the marital bed. Whether that is emotional or physical, it will not be healthy for your marriage.

If I could only give you one piece of advice, it would be this. If you have any friend of the opposite sex that gives you butterflies or excites you when you see each other, exit this relationship and find a way to draw closer to your spouse instead. Protect your marriage for no one else will but the two of you. All marriages must be protected from the inside out to withstand the trappings of this world. Those trappings seem to grow year after year, be on alert. Many will gladly take your spouse if you no longer treasure them.

If there has been infidelity within your marriage, I want to give you hope. I have worked with numerous marriages that have survived and thrived after affair recovery. Find a good counselor, be honest and transparent moving forward. Try to work out these issues with honesty and compassion for one another. Generally, when infidelity occurs, both parties are feeling the pain in the aftermath.

Infidelity does not have to become a death sentence for the marriage. I have seen many couples work through recovery from an affair and end up being closer and stronger afterward. If the adulterous relationship is over, then recovery is possible in the right environment.

Push through, do the work, get help if you need it. However, refuse to give up hope. Keep walking it out together and find your way back to a healthy bond and relationship.

COPING SKILLS

This book would not be complete without discussing coping skills. Coping skills are the methods we use to deal with frustrations, disappointments, and challenges of life. Once a challenge is presented, the way you deal with it is an indicator of your coping skills. What are your coping skills? What tools do you use in times of trouble? We all need healthy tools for managing challenges, stress, and tiredness. The time to prepare for a storm is not when it is hitting. The best time to prepare your disaster plan is before the storm even forms. The same is true with coping skills. It is important to have a few to try out before life's storms hit. It's best if you get ready by knowing what your tools are and how to use them prior to the challenges hitting your life.

Everyone's coping skills are different. Do not expect your coping skill to work for everyone else in your life. Find what works for you and don't try and make everyone else do it the same way. As I have aged, I have found each decade has added different coping tools to my toolbox of life skills. Each challenge I have experienced has led to new knowledge in methods to cope and communicate. The more tools you have, the more you are prepared to find a healthy way to cope.

Let us look at just a few; the gym, gardening, music, animals, faith, taking a bubble bath, bike riding, writing, reading, puzzles, cleaning, fidget spinners, etc. For some people, talking through the thoughts in their minds helps them to vent their frustrations or concerns, and they begin to feel better by simply discussing their problems. For other people, working out helps them by leaving the stress in a puddle of sweat on the gym floor. Some people use distractions to cope like video games, cleaning, or even work to redirect their minds in a different direction than their stressor. My husband has had times in his life he suffered from profound anxiety. He has learned from experience what works. Now when he feels it beginning, he can engage his coping skills, and the anxiety does not rule his life. I utilize scriptures and worship as my best coping skills. Scripture recall and repetition help strengthen my faith and remind me to trust the Lord. This is single-handedly my greatest personal coping skill. In a remarkably close second is playing worship music and praising the Lord. Life can be full of great trails, and I put on worship music (especially music that has scriptures in the song), and it refreshes my mind by redirecting my thinking patterns. Within a short time, my thinking turns to praise for all my blessings rather than focusing on my problems.

Music is mood-altering, be aware, just as great music can lift your thoughts, depressing music can bring depressing thoughts to your mind as well. Have you ever heard a song, and almost instantly, you are transported to a memory in your mind? Music is powerful to emotions, be careful with those sad songs if you are already feeling down. Instead, put on the music that will inspire you to worship and praise God for all the blessings in your life.

Different coping skills are good for different challenges. The tools that work at home may be completely different than the ones you need to cope with the challenges at work. The skills you utilize when you are getting along with your spouse are generally quite different than the ones you use when dealing with the stress from daily life.

There are countless books, podcasts, and teachings on coping skills. If you do not feel your toolbox is full of good tools, seek a wise counselor, read books, and research to continually grow and develop new skills. As your toolbox fills with coping skills and you learn to use them correctly, you will find less confusion, strife, and overload in your day-to-day life.

As a counselor, I need to share a special warning about the words we speak out of our own lips. The Bible warns, especially as women, to be aware of amounts and what we say on bad days. Remember the scripture about the foolish woman who tears down her own house with her own hands and her words from her own lips? Be on guard that you are not doing this to your own life. I can be kind or a nag to my husband. My mouth can be full of bitter words full of griping and complaining, or I can be gentle, full of love, and look for the positive instead.

For example, my husband makes the bed every day, and I know he does it for me. He does not do this because he needs to or wants to. He does this for me. It is a daily gift of love to me from him. He never seems to make it exactly as I do, the pillows aren't quite where I always put them, but I love to walk in the room and see the bed made. Again, he doesn't even care if the bed is made. It is completely done to make me happy. Now I have a choice, and I can complain or, worse, remake the bed so that it's to my standards of making the bed, or I can say thank you and show my appreciation. It's a choice I must make. I can gripe, explaining he's not doing it my way, and then maybe he never does it again. When doing this, I could lose this gift that he's been giving me of a made bed. Or I can walk in the room and see the bed is made, know he did it and see it as the gift of love he meant it to be, and thank him for his efforts. This is me choosing to look at the positive rather than the negative. This is me choosing to nurture our friendship and relationship rather than ripping it apart with my own hands and voice. I make an active choice to connect with my spouse rather than rejecting him with criticism.

> "It is better to live in a desert than with a quarrelsome and *nagging wife*" (Proverbs 21:19 Soul Care Bible).

Another version reads…

> "[It is] better to dwell in the wilderness, than with a contentious and an angry woman" (Proverbs 21:19 NIV).

> "A quarrelsome wife is like the dripping of a leaky roof in a rainstorm; restraining her is like restraining the wind or grasping oil with the hand" (Proverbs 27:15-16 NIV).

The Bible says a nagging wife will send her husband to the roof. This is exactly what it's talking about. If we nag about little things, we chase our spouse away from us, which is usually the opposite of what we're trying to do. He shows me love with acts of service because that's his love language. He shows me his love by making the bed, doing the dishes, and doing kind things for me. It is important that I recognize the acts of kindness from my spouse and truly reflect gratitude for it. There is an opportunity for gratitude in each day.

Where did you find yours today? Remember each of these moments brings us closer together, or they are processed as rejections, as we discussed in earlier chapters.

When I make an error, I ask for forgiveness or credit to my forgiveness account; when he makes an error, he gets credit to his account. We both almost always end up messing up the same amount, just in different ways. I forgive him of his mistakes, large and small, and he forgives mine. We take turns messing up and sometimes hurting each other's feelings unintentionally. These are moments that being quick to forgive and release offense brings and keeps peace within our marriage. I am not the one constantly forgiving him as I walk in perfection; I am only human, and even with a PhD, I still make the silliest mistakes and need him to forgive me rather often.

In the beginning of our marriage, forgiving was a lot more difficult. We were young and still really getting to know one another. We stepped on each other's toes and triggered each other often without even realizing it sometimes. Now, twenty years later, we know each other so well it is much easier to forgive and forget quickly. Forgiveness does get easier the more you do it. The more you let things go, the more you realize life is so much more peaceful without carrying around all the baggage of the mistakes of yesterday.

I met a weeping woman that shared her pain from being left by the love of her life. She was hurt, broken, and lonely. Her tears turned to rivers for all she had lost. She now could see things that she could not see before he left. She talked to me of all the times she had the opportunity to connect with him but did not. She shared all the nagging that occurred in her marriage and how he said, often, he couldn't do things right enough for her. He told her she saw him as a failure that could not do the simplest things correctly.

I challenge you to stop and see, open your eyes to what is around you. See the beauty but also see the pain and look at what is real so you may grow to the next level of your life and learn to appreciate the blessings that have been provided for you.

Build your spouse up at every opportunity available to you. There are plenty of people in this world ready to tear people down for their flaws. We should do everything possible to be our spouse's cheerleader. We should be their support, encouragement, and the one always there, ready to love and accept them no matter what. When this type of love is present in your home, it is a successful home and marriage.

Now let's take a different look at trust. I have heard people say, "I am such a fool for believing _____" (fill in the blank). The truth is, we can only really see things if our eyes are open if we are really watching things and paying attention to what is happening around us. When we trust and are hurt in return, we must learn to apply forgiveness to the situation. It does not mean we are foolish for believing. I choose to believe we are brave for trusting even knowing we stand a chance at being hurt.

Let's talk one more time about the watchmen on the wall for protection. The watchmen's job was to watch for and alert the town's people of oncoming attacks by the enemy. The purpose was to see the attacks far off when they came and alert everyone to be ready once they arrived. This was to alert every one of the attacks before a devastating assault. When you can see the attack before it happens, you have time to devise a defensive strategy. The point is we must be the watchmen on the walls of our home, family, church, and friendships. If your eyes are open and you are participating in your relationships, you will often see the oncoming attacks before they bring harm, and you can often prevent or at least prepare correctly. But this is only true if you are actively participating and watching for what is coming in your direction. This area is addressed time and time again in counseling offices across the nation. Participation is a requirement in all successful relationships. If all decisions, plans, protection, and work are made by just one member of the team, then bitterness grows inside the person that feels as if they are doing more of the work. A successful marriage has two active partners, trying to connect and stay connected on purpose.

We all take a turn at happy and sad. We all have ups, we all have downs. We all have happy days and sad days, times of sickness and times of good health. There are days that we are the caregiver for those we love, and there are also days where we need a caregiver to care for us. Friends and jobs come and go; life gives us U-turns with ups and downs. So, let's talk about unplanned life changes, accidents, and illnesses as well as the effects they have on our relationships.

In my marriage, we have had hospitalizations and ups and downs with illness from my husband's disability. There were times that I felt like I was the doing all the work with no relief in sight. Then there were days when my health failed where he took care of me and did all the work. In my darkest days of grief, when we lost my mom and best friend, my husband took unbelievably great care of me. He was kind and understanding. He would hold me as I wept, and he took care of the million little daily life things I had no patience or ability to handle. He truly was my caregiver during these times. I would not have made it through it all without his tender loving care. For the rest of my days, I will be so grateful to him for how he helped me with everything and the countless times he told me everything was going to be alright. He brought me such great security.

Be patient when it's your turn to be the giver. Rest assured the day comes when you will be the receiver of care. These times usually come when you least expect it or aren't prepared for it. Don't give up during the hard times, instead look for the Lord in everything and see what He is trying to teach you. Find your best you to approach each area of challenge.

To love means to stay when it's hard and never to give up. When we work hard at giving our best to our marriage, then we often can benefit from the spirit of reciprocity. This means you get a turn being both the giver and the receiver. One of our favorite Friends TV show episodes is when one of the characters, Joey, is writing vows for his friend's wedding, and he uses the words giving and receiving at least ten times. YouTube this episode it's great because really that is what a marriage is all about giving and receiving, receiving, and giving, giving and receiving. This cycle of giving and receiving should be unending in our marriages.

Helping you understand how to hold on to your marriage and keep it alive when it is hard or when you are deeply in need is why this book was written. The foundation to success has often been traced back to the art of forgiving one another. There are times when we need someone to forgive us for things we say or do because not one of us is perfect. The day is coming, which I must admit happens more often than I'd like, that I will need to ask my husband to forgive me, and I will really want him to quickly and completely forgive me for whatever mistake I made. If I need him to forgive me my faults, then I must forgive him of his faults as well.

Forgiveness, when given freely and completely, is where healing and restoration can truly begin. I believe this process applies not only in our marriage but to all relationships in some form. This includes our children, grandchildren, parents, and those select few you are allowed to be your family even beyond these boundaries. Forgiveness is the key to freedom from the bitterness and resentment that chokes the life from your heart and spirit. If you have the key in your hand, my friend, use it!

Resentment can turn into bitterness, and then bitterness can turn into walls that prevent true connection in your relationships. This is a direct ticket to isolation, and that is the opposite of how God designed love to operate.

There have been periods in my marriage that I held so many hurt feelings and anger inside. I watered them with unforgiveness and then was shocked that we were sleeping in separate bedrooms or responding to one another like roommates rather than best friends. In that season, we almost lost each other due to the growing resentment and bitterness that birthed such separation of our hearts. During this time, we found it to be difficult to connect or come into unity for even the simplest things. We were so isolated from one another.

Let this be a warning to you when you feel the bitterness in your heart, be quick to pray and heal those feelings to prevent isolation from taking hold in your home. I have heard so many people say I feel so lonely in my marriage. This is where that loneliness begins…in bitterness and resentment separating you from your partner in life. It is through learning and practicing forgiveness that we find our way back to closeness, unity, and real Godly love.

Not long ago, I was having lunch with a wonderful friend that I treasure, and she shared something that really touched me. She said, "I cannot wait until I get to be a wife. I pray for this blessing every day." Instantly I thought of the days in the beginning when I was head over heels in love with my husband, who is my soul mate, and it started this self-examination that went on for days. When was the last time I celebrated the fact I get to be his wife rather than his widow? When was the last time that I celebrated that I am the mother of the best-looking smartest sons and most beautiful daughter there are in this world? Or even the last time I was grateful for the job, I have spent a lifetime praying into being? Sometimes we live in the house we have always wanted but complain when it is time to clean it or paint it or repair it. We should be thankful, grateful, and happy for these such blessings. These blessings that we really want in our lives come with work or maintenance on our parts.

Sometimes with our husbands and/or children that are blessings, we need to exercise the ability to forgive and not tire in doing good to and with them. What we give into our families will affect the health of the family.

People used to always say the grass is greener on the other side. I say the grass is greener wherever you water and fertilize it. If you want to have a green yard, you must water it, and you must feed the grass with fertilizer. This also holds true with your relationships, especially your marriage. If you want the love to grow in your marriage, then you must feed it. If we want a beautiful yard, we have to kill the weeds. Same with your marriage, be alert to examine what the weeds are in your marriage. Is it careless talk, hateful words, sassy mouths, disrespect, ignoring one another with the silent treatment, or even sarcastic comments?

My husband and I went from roommates to lovers to best friends and, with work and maintenance to renew friendship, also administering gallons and gallons of forgiveness. This is the formula that works for a successful marriage. We must hold on to the key of friendship with both hands, refusing to let friendship slowly slip out of the relationship. It seems the world fights to keep you from being best friends, but that is how you make it through all the good and all the bad and all the really bad times. It is by holding on to your best friend's hand and both of you agreeing, "it's me and you against the world."

I have learned the hard way that when you are hurting, take time to work through it before you share your pain with others. If you do not know what to do, then just be still, take a breath, calm your nerves, then think of the options and wait until your brain is through the magnitude of the stress. Wait until the ideas and reasoning begin to flow again. When you're upset, angry, and hurt, be still and try to keep your voice quiet, focus before you respond. So often, we speak out of our pain and then deeply regret what we said. Do not let this happen to you.

An especially important mentor in my life taught me, "hurting people hurt people." When a person is in pain, they will often lash out at others, sometimes without even understanding what they are doing. When our heart hurts, when our emotions are out of control, that is when we need to be on guard of what words come out of our mouths. Pain and anger are very great fuels that can cause very heated fires. This can cause severe and often long-term pain.

A parent wearies from the challenges of their day. If not on guard, they can easily blow their frustrations on a child who is not behaving as the parent wishes. This can also happen with spouses; we come home from a long day of work frustrated and aggravated from all the stresses of the day or from fighting traffic, and within minutes we can become enthralled in an argument with our spouse.

If not careful in those moments of frustration, we can begin taking it out on our partner. When the truth is, we are the one who needs to take a time out to get our thoughts collected before venting or speaking and sharing the frustration with someone who does not deserve it. I often recommend to people that I see in the counseling office that when you walk through the door at the end of a long, frustrating day, the best thing you can do is be alone for ten to fifteen minutes to calm yourself before you let any of your frustrations exit your lips.

We must be on guard when anger, frustration, or even tiredness is bubbling up within us. We would do better to say nothing at all and take time to cool off rather than blow up, harm another, and then ask for forgiveness later. This sounds like such a simple thing, but it is so important not to vent our frustrations on our spouse. I agree that talking things out with your partner in life is a particularly good coping skill. However, I recommend cooling your emotions prior to talking it out so that your partner does not feel attacked or triggered by your emotions. If this is ignored very quickly, you can double your frustrations and have your partner frustrated with you as well.

Several years ago, in our youth, my husband and I were experiencing a year of challenges that came to a total of four hospitalizations, amongst other dilemmas going on at the same time. Our marriage successfully survived due to the third strand of our cord that ties us to one another in our marriage. The Lord caused so many circumstances to keep my husband and I together when we were in our seasons of difficulty. There were times we thought we were ready to walk away from our commitment to one another. We were surrounded by supports and challenges that made a split too difficult to happen. The Lord kept us connected in impossible ways until we learned to love each other again.

When we did not desire to be together, the Lord kept us together until we could not live without each other once again. He made a way to keep us together even when we did not know that was what we really wanted in the depths of our hearts. God is good, and He is faithful even when we are not and do not deserve it. During these times, I cannot count how many times I cried out to God to help us stay together and recover from our pain. He knew what was best for me. He was the third strand that strengthened our cord and kept us together.

> For I know the plans I have for you,"
> declares the LORD, "plans to prosper you
> and not to harm you, plans to give you
> hope and a future. Then you will call on
> me and come and pray to me, and I will
> listen to you. You will seek me and find
> me when you seek me with all your heart.
> Jeremiah 29:11-13 (NIV)

Even when I did not know what was best for my life, the Lord did. Because after we traveled a long hard road, we made it to the other side, and I firmly know my husband is the love of my life. Now I pray and give great thanksgiving to God for keeping us together. That third strand of our cord is the Lord. When it is as bad as it gets, and you remain faithful and invested, the challenges will take the marriage to a whole new level on the other side of the trials. God holds us tightly together. A cord that has three strands is not easily broken; this means when it is so hard for you to hold onto each other, the Lord holds you together with *His* power and truth.

I have watched marriages die due to not having the strength of the third cord. When it's just you and your spouse, and you are trying to handle the resistance of real life in this world, it is easy to become weak and tired. If you live and walk in your own power and wisdom, it is easy for your strength to dwindle, your resolve to fade, and then you start wondering why you are staying in your relationship. It is almost impossible to get all your needs met and have all the supports you need present without the help of the Lord.

When experiencing the challenging years, there's a support system that will assist with marital success if God is in your hearts. The Lord can cause situations and circumstances to cause forgiveness and love to happen just when needed to help us hold on to our covenant of marriage. So, the real answer to how to hold on is to seek the Lord and follow His guidance and wisdom. We must invite the Lord to be a part of our marriages. Then He provides the way where there seems to be no way.

There was a day I thought I was sure I wanted out of my marriage. I was terribly hurt and tired. But God showed me the truth. I would have missed so much if we had walked away and given up. If we had given up and ended our marriage, then the blessings would have been robbed from us. I am incredibly happy to report our life is so wonderful now. Our love is deeper, and our world is better due to all we came through together. Each hard season you walk through together helps your love grow stronger and stronger. These hard times, as we look back, we found they made our love greater.

The trials and challenges prove our three-stranded cord is strong and anointed with the power to overcome all that has been or ever will be thrown at us. I would be at fault if I didn't take the time to state—God is no respecter of persons, and what He has done for us, He will do for you; all you need to do is ask Him to guide your relationship to healing and restoration and then believe He can and will do it. Because we did not let go in those hardest moments that should have broken us, we now praise God and give Him all the glory for our success. He renewed the love we have for one another in our hearts, and we are so thankful today for that deep and true love.

LAST THOUGHTS

Now let us talk about this "in love" stuff. There are huge differences between loving someone, being "in love," and lusting for someone. All three of these are possible within your marriage. Lust is generally a temporary season; some seasons last longer, and some are short, but you must know only true love lasts. It lasts because it is the love that chooses to continue to love even when things get difficult.

In Love is that mushy, heart-thumping, new car smell we often feel at the beginning of a relationship. This is a feeling that comes and goes many times in long-term successful marriages. It ebbs and tides, rolls in and rolls out several times during the life of a marriage. Do not ruin your marriage because you are no longer "in love"; you see, my friend, in love is not a requirement. It is a bonus. True love lasts beyond in love, and it is a constant no matter how you are feeling. True love is not a feeling. It is a choice. In love comes and goes at different stages in your marriage and will ebb and flow like the tide. Friendship can often come and go the same way. But if you allow it to, it always returns.

> Love is patient, love is kind. It does not
> envy, it does not boast, it is not proud.
> It does not dishonor others, it is not
> self-seeking, it is not easily angered, it
> keeps no record of wrongs. Love does not

delight in evil but rejoices with the truth.
It always protects, always trusts, always
hopes, always perseveres. Love never fails.
But where there are prophecies, they will
cease; where there are tongues, they will
be stilled; where there is knowledge, it
will pass away.

1 Corinthians 13:4-8 (NIV)

Do you still have fun together? This is such an important factor that is so often left neglected if not pursued with
intent. I often recommend to those in marriage counseling
to start engaging in routine date nights. You do not have
to commit to every week; every other week or even once a
month may work for your relationship. However, if closeness
has already drifted, then I would highly recommend for you
to start with a once-a-week date. A date can be the standard
dinner and a movie. I know for years when the kids were
much younger, we joked our date night was going out to eat
then going to Walmart to do our shopping. Even Walmart
can be fun if you are with the one you love. We would joke
and play as we did our shopping. The factor that mattered
most was we were alone together, having fun and igniting
our friendship.

If a relationship is not cared for and maintained, it can
suffer awful consequences. Remind yourself it is important for
your spouse to feel your interest and concern for what is going
on with them. We must engage and connect routinely in areas
other than chores, kids, and finances. How many friendships
are kept alive with no effort or fun? Please remind yourself
regularly marriage is more than the day-to-day requirements.
Marriage also consists of a multitude of moments you "get to
do," not just all the things you "have to do."

The problem I see time and time again in suffering relationships is we do the "have to" things with our mate then try to do the "get to" things with our other friends. This is problematic for marriage. Because with time, it can make your spouse a "have to" instead of the "want to" they are supposed to be. This is a choice that you are making every day, even if you are unaware you are making it. Your daily choices have consequences on the success of your relationship. We must choose one another as a priority in our everyday lives. Is your spouse your true partner in life? Is he or she one of your best friends? If not, why aren't they? What steps can you take to make a change in this area?

I believe guys need guy friends, and women need at least one good woman friend to talk things out and vent their feelings. However, I strongly believe your spouse should remain your best friend. When this area slips, then troubles begin. I understand in some relationships, the years can take their toll, and friendship can slowly slip away. If this is where you find your marriage right now, please let me encourage you to try and make a change. Try to reignite the friendship you once had.

You can become friends again. This generally will not happen overnight just because today you decided that is the direction you want to go. If you have not been maintaining your yard for a long time, then you will have some work to do pruning and pulling weeds for it to become beautiful again. This is the same idea with your marital relationship. Maybe it is time for you to pull the weeds of distraction, tiredness, resentment, and unforgiveness. Prune away all the hurtful memories of all the times things did not go right. And fertilize the garden of your marriage with love, friendship, understanding, forgiveness, and good old fashion fun. If you do this *consistently*, you will see your marriage transform into something so beautiful, everyone around you will ask you how you did it.

So, start today, make the decision to put effort into getting your friendship back by setting aside time for meaningful connections with one another. Show your partner love and forgiveness for everything that did not go like you planned or wanted it to go. Release the pain of the past and reach towards the promise of peace and friendship in your future.

If, at first, it does not work automatically and quickly, please stay with it. Do not give up. Refuse to quit. With time and consistency, you will see a change. I must stress the consistency element to this technique. It may take a moment or two to heal the hurts of yesterday before your newfound (or found again) friendship can flourish.

The important thing is to think about how to reignite your friendship with your spouse. When trying to restore life to your relationship, ask the Lord for guidance, speak positively over your relationship until you see it come into existence. The power of life and death is in your tongue. So, speak positivity over your relationship. Speak that you are kind and helpful to one another, that you are happy and growing together to be the best you can be to one another.

There was a time in our life together that I would call my husband "The King of all the asses that lived on the planet." I would sarcastically joke with him about him being a huge ass. Until one day, I heard a wonderful pastor speak about the power of death and life being in your tongue.

I decided that day I would be much more careful what I allowed to come out of my mouth. That day I decided I would call my husband "lover" instead of king of the asses. I must share with you just by me changing what I called him also very quickly changed how I saw him and then how he responded to me. Day after day, my choosing to call him my lover instead of the king reminded me he really was my lover, and we treat our lover differently, kinder, more lovingly, and I must add with a higher level of respect as well. When I called him king of asses, I saw him as an ass; but as I began to call him my lover, I saw him as just that. My words did change my perception that in turn changed my method of reacting to him. It also had a major effect on the perception of how he viewed my vision of who he was in my life.

Be more aware of how you talk about one another and your relationship in general. Carefully choose the words your release from your lips; be sure you are both speaking life into your home, marriage, and future. Be gentle with one another, be concerned about hurting your partner's feelings. Choose your pet names for one another carefully, especially the ones you use when you are aggravated.

It is important that you know yourself well. You must know what your needs and wants are, and this includes both expressed and expected needs. The more real you become with yourself, the more you can share with your partner. It is time to end the exhausting art of chasing approval or acceptance from others and begin to learn to love the real authentic you. You must be okay with who you are and be able to clearly communicate the true you to your partner.

There is such importance in you taking responsibility for your feelings, wants, and needs and learning to communicate them clearly. Then both of you can understand what is needed and expected of them. If you do not know who you are and what you need, how can you expect your partner to know you? When we are functioning in the wisdom of truly knowing and accepting our real authentic self, we can then give our partner the ability to understand us more clearly. In my own experience, this has only been achievable when the

Lord was in my life. He gives us a better vision of ourselves than any mirror ever could.

I spent so many years of my youth with anxiety and cravings for acceptance and love. To have that time back would be a gift. I didn't know who I was or what I needed to be happy. I did the work on myself to discover what I needed and wanted out of my life. I learned my triggers, coping skills, and reasons why I communicate the ways I do. I sometimes wondered if we would ever understand each other, but by the grace and mercy and forgiving power of God, here we are, still loving one another. We accept each other for exactly where we are in life. We learned about ourselves and invested time in hearing each other express what they need to be happy and fulfilled in life. We have learned how to meet one another at our point of need and communicate effectively.

Daily routines are more important than you may understand, especially when it is life maintenance. Just as we care for our vehicle or air conditioner, we must do routine maintenance on our marriages as well. Are you praying together? Are you spending time together? Are you growing together? Are you connecting or rejecting one another?

Love even when you do not feel like it. Try to understand the other person's pain and point of view even when you are hurting. Love even when you do not feel it coming back to you. Love as if all you do is for Jesus himself. Give even when they do not give back. Pray for your spouse and the marriage you dream of having. And while you wait for those prayers to be answered by the Lord, try working on you becoming the best partner you can be for your spouse. We are all works in progress so let us commit to progressing and not stopping the growth we need. This is a perfect time to begin, so start now.

I claim the success of our twenty-year marriage by the blessing and leadership of God. If He isn't the center of your home, that is the first place you can start. Ask Jesus into your heart, receive Him as your savior. Begin seeking a real relationship with God. Study the word of God together on a regular, consistent basis. This is the secret to a tremendously successful marriage. My prayer for your family and home is that you begin this journey today.

SCRIPTURE LIST

Dear friends, let us love one another, for love comes from God. Everyone who loves has been born of God and knows God. Whoever does not love does not know God, because God is love.

1 John 4:7-8 (NIV)

"For even when we were with you, we gave you this rule: "The one who is unwilling to work shall not eat" (2 Thessalonians 3:10 NIV)

And be ye kind one to another, tender-hearted, forgiving one another, even as God for Christ's sake hath forgiven you" (Ephesians 4:32 KJV)

Judge not, that ye be not judged. For with what judgment ye judge, ye shall be judged: and with what measure ye mete, it shall be measured to you again. And why beholdest thou the mote that is in thy brother's eye, but considerest not the beam that is in thine own eye? Or how wilt thou say to thy brother, let me pull out the mote out of thine eye; and behold, a beam *is* in thine own eye?

Matthew 7:1-4 (KJV)

I want to know Christ-yes, to know the power of his resurrection and participation in his sufferings, becoming like him in his death, and so, somehow, attaining to the resurrection from the dead. Not that I have already obtained all this, or have already arrived at my goal, but I press on to take hold of that for which Christ Jesus took hold of me. Brothers and sisters, I do not consider myself yet to have taken hold of it. But one thing I do: Forgetting what is behind and straining toward what is ahead, I press on toward the goal to win the prize for which God has called me heavenward in Christ Jesus.

Philippians 3: 10-14 (NIV)

Whatever is true, whatever is honorable, whatever is just, whatever is pure, whatever is lovely, whatever is commendable, if there is ANY excellence, if there is anything worthy of praise, think about these things.

Philippians 4:19 NIV

We destroy arguments and every lofty opinion raised against the knowledge of God, and take every thought captive to obey Christ" (2 Corinthians10:5 ESV)

Whoever sows sparingly will also reap sparingly, and whoever sows generously will also reap generously. Each of you should give what you have decided in your heart to give, not reluctantly or under compulsion, for God loves a cheerful giver. And God is able to bless you abundantly, so that in all things at all times, having all that you need, you will abound in every good work.

2 Corinthians 9:6-8 6 (NIV)

"The tongue can bring death or life; those who love to talk will reap the consequences" (Proverbs 18:21 NLT)

Lay not up for yourselves treasures upon earth, where moth and rust doth corrupt, and where thieves break through and steal: But lay up for yourselves treasures in heaven, where neither moth nor rust doth corrupt, and where thieves do not break through nor steal: For where your treasure is, there will your heart be also.

Mathew 6: 19-21 (NIV)

If thy brother shall trespass against thee, go, and tell him his fault between thee and him alone: if he shall hear thee, thou hast gained thy brother. But if he will not hear thee, then take with thee one or two more, that in the mouth of two or three witnesses every word may be established.

And if he shall neglect to hear them, tell it unto the church: but if he neglects to hear the church, let him be unto thee as a heathen man and a publican. Verily I say unto you, Whatsoever ye shall bind on earth shall be bound in heaven: and whatsoever ye shall loose on earth shall be loosed in heaven. Again, I say unto you, that if two of you shall agree on earth as touching anything that they shall ask, it shall be done for them of my Father which is in heaven. For where two or three are gathered together in my name, there am I in the midst of them.

Mathew 18:15-20 (KJV)

Every wise woman buildeth her house: but the foolish plucketh it down with her hands. He that walketh in his uprightness feareth the LORD: but he that is perverse in his ways despises him. In the mouth of the foolish is a rod of pride: but the lips of the wise shall preserve them.

Proverbs 14:1 (KJV)

So do not worry, saying, 'What shall we eat?' or 'What shall we drink?' or 'What shall we wear?' For the pagans run after all these things, and your heavenly Father knows that you need them. But seek first his kingdom and his righteousness, and all these things will be given to you as well.

Matthew 6:31-33 (NIV)

"Therefore a man shall leave his father and his mother and hold fast to his wife, and the two shall become one flesh" (Matthew 19:5 ESV)

"And though a man might prevail against one who is alone, two will withstand him-a threefold cord is not quickly broken" (Ecclesiastes 4:12 ESV)

The husband should fulfill his marital duty to his wife, and likewise the wife to her husband. The wife does not have authority over her own body but yields it to her husband. In the same way, the husband does not have authority over his own body but yields it to his wife. Do not deprive each other except perhaps by mutual consent and for a time, so that you may devote yourselves to prayer. Then come together again so that Satan will not tempt you because of your lack of self-control.
1 Corinthians 7:3-5 (NIV)

"[It is] better to dwell in a corner of the housetop, than with a brawling woman in a wide house" (Proverbs 21:9 NIV)

"[It is] better to dwell in the wilderness, than with a contentious and an angry woman" (Proverbs 21:19 NIV)

For I know the plans I have for you," declares the LORD, "plans to prosper you and not to harm you, plans to give you hope and a future. Then you will call on me and come and pray to me, and I will listen to you. You will seek me and find me when you seek me with all your heart.

Jeremiah 29:11-13 (NIV)

Love is patient, love is kind. It does not envy, it does not boast, it is not proud. It does not dishonor others, it is not self-seeking, it is not easily angered, it keeps no record of wrongs. Love does not delight in evil but rejoices with the truth. It always protects, always trusts, always hopes, always perseveres. Love never fails. But where there are prophecies, they will cease; where there are tongues, they will be stilled; where there is knowledge, it will pass away.

1 Corinthians 13:4-8 (NIV)

CPSIA information can be obtained
at www.ICGtesting.com
Printed in the USA
FSHW011437260321
79778FS